**Other topics covered in this series**

Fishkeeping
Railway Modelling
Stamp Collecting

Birdwatching in the rain!

# How About Birdwatching

by

## Val Singleton

and

## Arthur Gilpin

ep

EP Publishing Limited

## Acknowledgements

The frontispiece and photographs on pages 12 and 17 were taken by Jonathan Smith. All the other photographs are by Arthur Gilpin, including the cover, which shows puffins at the Farne Islands.

The layout and graphics are by Ray Williams.

## ISBN o 7158 o653 X

Published by EP Publishing Ltd, East Ardsley, Wakefield, West Yorkshire, 1979

Printed in Great Britain by
Fletcher & Son Ltd, Norwich

## The Authors

VALERIE SINGLETON trained as an actress at the Royal Academy of Dramatic Art before becoming one of the main presenters of 'Blue Peter', the most successful British children's programme. From 'Blue Peter' she moved on to 'Tonight', the news digest at peak viewing time.

ARTHUR GILPIN is a veteran birdwatcher who has specialised in bird photography, for which he has been awarded an honorary M.Sc. by Leeds University. His previous writing includes two books, *Know the Game: Birdwatching* and *Nature Photography*, both published by EP Publishing. Arthur Gilpin has been secretary and president of several ornithological and nature photographic societies.

# Contents

# 1  BIRDWATCHING AS A HOBBY
## by Val Singleton

Watching birds is a fascinating hobby that has one great advantage – you can do it almost anywhere. Just keep your eyes open, be observant and you will be surprised how many birds you can see, wherever you live. They are all around you.

Do you live in a town or city? Well, many birds live above you in the high buildings where you can see them perched on ledges or maybe making their nests under overhanging roofs. Go out to the parks, church-yards and squares and look up into the trees; even in streets that seem to have no greenery you will often spot a blackbird singing on a rooftop.

Where I live now, right in the heart of London, besides sparrows there are several raucous rooks, two very colourful and noisy jays, and in the summer swifts dart about in the late evening air catching insects. In spring a blackbird sings quite beautifully, and sometimes a thrush turns up. I have a small balcony on to which some birds come to eat scraps I put out for them. Among these visitors is my favourite, a tame pigeon I have nicknamed Pidge. On rare occasions I have heard the magnificent sound of swans in flight, and have rushed out just in time to watch them fly over the house. Then at night I often hear the cry of an owl, and sometimes I have even seen the outline of it in the dark perched in a tree. Yes, there are plenty of birds to be seen in the very centre of the city!

Wherever you live there is so much to learn about birds – about their behaviour, their varied songs, the different plumage of each species and how it changes through the year. You will notice that some birds appear and disappear at different seasons and this may lead you on to discover the fascinating story of migration – of which birds travel to and from other countries and why they do so. The more you get to know about birds the more absorbing the hobby becomes, and you may well find yourself involved for many happy hours. There are also ways to go about your chosen hobby that will make it easier and more rewarding.

It was to find out about some of these things that I journeyed north to spend the day with the well-known ornithologist, Arthur Gilpin. Arthur's interest in the hobby started over sixty years ago when he was about eight. Up on the Ridge above Meanwood in Leeds he learned the differences between the songs of mistle and song thrushes; down at his father's allot-ment were a variety of birds attracted by the plentiful supply of food.

7

They were called by names that you will not find in modern fieldguides; a hedge sparrow, for instance, was known to Yorkshiremen as a 'cuddy'.

Arthur went on to pursue his hobby as an accompaniment to a varied life that has taken him to many parts of the world. In particular he concentrated on bird photography, and the photographs taken by him that are included in this book testify to the skill and patience he must have needed. He has gone on to write many articles and books on the subject.

Patience is a quality you really must have if you are to become a successful birdwatcher. You will often have to remain still for long periods – but if you do have patience and are truly interested, the moment when your waiting is rewarded is worth every minute. Arthur told me that he is always so enthralled with what is taking place around him that he never notices time passing.

It is also important that you should have an appreciation of wild life in general; in fact you will hardly be able to avoid developing one. Many species have their own particular range of habitats, whether this is reed-bed, conifer woodland, open heath or some other. A knowledge of the plants or insects on which birds feed is one of the keys to understanding the birds themselves; a knowledge of geology and climate will help you learn about habitats. Soon it will all fit together and your hobby will have opened up for you the exciting pattern of natural history.

## Around the home

If you live in the country or near the sea your opportunities for observing a wide variety of birds will be greater than those of towndwellers. But wherever you live if you have a garden or are lucky enough to be able to see trees, one of the best places to begin your study of birds is from the windows of your own home. This can be very useful, too, if you are ill for any length of time or are unable to move about outside freely.

The secret is to attract the birds to your home, and there are many ways in which you can go about this. First give some thought to the plants you grow. Many birds love to eat berries, so berry-producing shrubs can be a great draw. Among these are cotoneaster and hawthorn – some of the birds that come in the winter are very fond of their fruits.

Whether or not you can plant the best shrubs, almost everyone can manage some sort of a bird table which you can either buy or make for yourself. Remember to fix it well out of the way of cats, and it is also a good idea to arrange some sort of cover so that predators find it harder to pounce and the food is kept dry. You can buy grain hoppers or seed dispensers to hang on your table, or again, you could make your own.

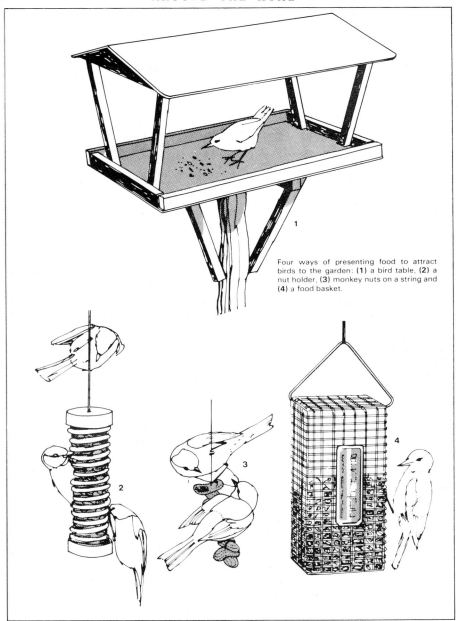

Four ways of presenting food to attract birds to the garden: (1) a bird table, (2) a nut holder, (3) monkey nuts on a string and (4) a food basket.

Arthur Gilpin also told me of a way of having a pulley system arranged between your window and a tree or post so that if you are stuck indoors you can still operate the table.

Great tit

Putting out water is most important. At times of drought or during severe frosts your supply may mean the difference between life and death to some birds. One word of warning: never put glycerine in the water to stop it freezing, as this is very bad for the birds. It is much better to change the water every day. Among solid foods that birds like are nuts and seeds, bacon rind, left-over meat, suet, bread, cheese, rotten apples and other household scraps. They will also appreciate a sort of cake made of different foods bound together with melted fat and sliced when it has hardened. A more expensive way of feeding is to buy ready-prepared mixtures. You can put out food all the year round and you will be surprised at the variety of birds that will be attracted to your garden. Particularly pretty, perhaps, are the blue- and great tits that show a superb sense of balance as they cling to the bottom of a swaying nut-bag. The period from the end of October until the beginning of April is the time when your bird-table will be most appreciated. Be careful what you put out when birds are feeding their young: very fatty or starchy foods can be bad for nestlings.

Another way of bringing birds to your own garden is to put up a nest-box. Then you can follow the course of its occupation from the time it is first chosen by the adult pair and lined with grass or feathers to the time when the brood leaves the nest. Do not remove the box cover to look in until you see the adults carrying food to the young. Even then to do so too frequently may cause the parents to desert, or the nestlings to leave the nest before they are fit to do so.

## Visiting a reserve

There are some five hundred species of birds in Britain, and although you can attract many to your garden and observe them there at close quarters, you will probably also feel the urge to progress farther afield. This might well mean quite a lot of walking, so you must enjoy being outdoors and not mind a bit of rain or the cold – or the reverse, days up in the hills with little shelter from a hot sun.

The day I spent with Arthur was very windy and wet, but it was surprising how quickly I forgot about the weather. I was much too absorbed in wondering what bird I was going to see next. I quickly discovered that you need good eyesight. We spent most of our day in a wooden hide among trees on the edge of a small lake. The day was dark and the canopy of trees further obscured our view. The lake itself was dark brown, and growing from it were reeds and willows. Old stumps lay

Going up to a hide at Adel Dam nature reserve, near Leeds

in the water. Canada geese were easy to see as they glided along, their black necks and white faces showing clearly against the green reeds. But when a medium-sized, blackish bird began to feed at the muddy edge of a small island it was much more difficult to tell whether it was a coot or a moorhen. Your eyesight can be aided by the use of binoculars, possibly the largest outlay you will ever have to make for this hobby. As I said earlier, Arthur started birdwatching when he was eight. He was nineteen and had already had great enjoyment from the activity before he bought his own first pair of binoculars; so it is quite possible to do without them. However, they do make a lot of difference if you really want to see all the details of a bird's plumage. You can share binoculars, buy them second-hand, or get a new pair: how much you spend is really up to you. Although you will make sure how keen you are before you rush out and spend your money, once you have acquired your 'glasses' they will last for ever – unless of course you drop or lose them.

Almost as important as eyesight is a retentive ear for birdsong and calls. Not only will sound sometimes alert you to a bird's presence – think, for

The view of the Adel Dam lake on a summer's day

instance, how far the cuckoo's call can be heard – but it will often be one of the best ways to differentiate between species.

Arthur was wearing a brown anorak with plenty of pockets, and when you choose what clothes to wear the most important thing to remember is that their colours should be subdued. In built-up areas and parks birds may not be so shy of humans, in the wilds of the country it is a very different matter. You must wear something that will merge fairly well with your background so that when you are stalking a bird or sitting quietly you will not be too noticeable. Of course, your clothes should also be weatherproof if you are going to be outdoors for any length of time.

It takes time to build up your knowledge of birds to the point where you can be confident of identifying every species. Invaluable while you learn will be a pocket-sized fieldguide to birds like the one included in this book from page 42. There are many excellent books available, and a list of suitable ones will be found on page 37. Among the information given by a guide is the birds' habitats, their size, colour, song and range. By 'range' is meant in what parts of the country the bird is likely to be found and this may be different from 'habitat'. Thus although there are woods throughout Britain and the nightingale inhabits woods, nonetheless it is seldom to be found north of the Humber. Books, then, are most important, and the more you read the more you will begin to understand your subject; something you can do on long winter evenings.

Suitable clothing, binoculars and fieldguide almost complete your birdwatching equipment but there is just one more indispensable aid . . . a pocket notebook. Among the items you should note are date, time of day and precise location. Then describe the weather and what sort of site you are at – whether, for instance, it is woodland, moorland or seashore. Having set the scene you can then make a note of what birds you see. There may be something unusual about the behaviour of one of the birds; write down precisely what you are lucky enough to observe. But at the same time do not forget what you think are just ordinary ocurrences; when you get home you can enter all these items into a larger book and over the years you will begin to build up the data that may be valuable information on bird behaviour. Among the observations you can record are the arrival and departure of migrants, like the first cuckoo or the last swallow. It is careful observations and recordings like this that have allowed us to check mistaken beliefs about natural history; here for instance are a few lines of what Gilbert White of Selborne wrote in 1777, a time when many assumptions about bird behaviour – in this case whether martins hibernated or migrated – were being tested:

'It appears by my journals for many years past that house martins retire, to a Bird, about the beginning of October; so that a person not very observant of such matters would conclude that they had taken their last farewell; but then it may be seen in my diaries also that considerable flocks have discovered themselves again in the first week of November . . . playing at their leisure and feeding calmly. . . .'

So, you record facts, both routine and unusual, about the birds you know; but you will also come across birds that are strange to you. If you are unable to recognise a bird, the more that you can write down about it, the more help you will have given yourself in identifying it later. Here are some pointers: see if it reminds you of a bird you already know; say whether it is larger or smaller; note its shape, markings and colour; see the kind of bill it has and note whether its legs are long, short or medium; look for anything distinctive about its feet. Watching the bird in flight may tell you a lot about what it might be; and another valuable help will be its song. Finally, you may feel able to sketch the bird. All these features are illustrated or described in the good fieldguides so that you can relate your notes to the guide and see how well they match. This should lead you to identifying your bird for certain. After a few days looking at the various details of a bird you will be amazed at how much more observant you will have become.

Once you have acquired your notebook, fieldguide and – possibly –

| Puzzles Dam 29/1/78 | Dry, sunny and cold | Wind light and north easterly |
|---|---|---|

| Birds seen | Totals | Notes |
|---|---|---|
| **In the wood:** | | |
| Robin 1,1 | 2 | They were in different parts of the wood. |
| Tawny Owl 1 | 1 | Roosting in the beech tree nesting box. |
| Blackbird ♂,♂. ♀ | 2♂ 1♀ | They were all turning over leaves under the trees. |
| Song Thrush 1 | 1 | |
| Mistle Thrush 1 | 1 | Singing in a tall tree. |
| Wren 1,1 | 2 | |
| Great Tit 1,1 | 2 | |
| Blue Tit 1 | 1 | |
| Long-tailed Tit 8 | 8 | This was a family party flying from tree to tree. |
| **From the lake hide:** | | |
| Coot 2 | 2 | They were bringing weeds to the surface. |
| Mallard 5♂ 6♀ | 5♂ 6♀ | |
| Teal 3♂ 5♀ | 3♂ 5♀ | I could hear others piping in the reeds |
| Tufted Duck 2♂ 3♀ | 2♂ 3♀ | They were diving constantly. |

\*There was a diving duck I had not seen before. In size between the Mallard and Teal, it had a much more receding forehead than the Tufted Duck

\* A sample of a field notebook. The unidentified bird was a drake Pochard.

pair of binoculars, you will find that you are well on the way to becoming a serious and dedicated birdwatcher. Now will be the time to explore new territory. Around the country and often on the edges of our towns (as with the reserve near Leeds I visited with Arthur Gilpin) there are many bird reserves and wildlife sanctuaries, undisturbed areas of land where the birds are free to pursue their lives free of unexpected intrusions. These are ideal places for the less experienced birdwatcher to visit.

The reserve near Leeds is protected by a high wooden fence. To enter you need to obtain a key from the Yorkshire Naturalists' Trust and let yourself in through the gate. A series of tracks run through the woodland and across the marsh to two 'hides' placed on the edge of the lake. A hide is just what it sounds like – a place for you to hide yourself so that the birds will be unaware of human presence. These particular ones were long huts solidly built of dark timber that merged with the background. They were also raised up quite high so that you could look down and across at the water. The huts could hold maybe eight or ten people, sitting on benches provided. At head height was a row of windows, each with its own trapdoor which you opened inwards so that you could see out. The one important thing to remember is not to poke your hand or your binoculars out beyond the slots; this will frighten the birds. And, of course, we all kept as quiet as possible.

I found on that wet, windy day that it was a good idea to have a thermos flask of hot coffee or soup. Sitting quietly for several hours can give you very cold toes!

Other reserves make different arrangements about hides. On some you will find access to hides on the edge of the reserve free and open to everyone, and inside them guides to the special birds you are most likely to see; at others you may have to pay or make arrangements with a local warden. In a few of the more elaborate hides, particularly those run by the World Wildlife Fund, the slots are covered in plate glass and the whole hide protected by acoustic material. Most, though, are similar to the ones at Leeds I have described.

In many cases the reserves will be in places where particularly exciting sights are to be seen – huge flocks of waders on the coast, for instance. A visit to one of these reserves can easily be the highlight of a holiday for all the family, however keen each individual might be on birdwatching as a hobby.

Away from the reserve there is nothing to stop you setting up your own hide. There are many different kinds of hide, the simplest being a one-person canvas tent. Rather surprisingly a car makes a good hide: it is

'. . . a good idea to have a thermos flask of hot coffee'

mobile, and quite effective so long as you remember to remain inside and do not let anything protrude through the windows.

## Birdsong

One of the great pleasures of birdwatching is that it can be enjoyed in any month of the year and almost all the hours of the day. Particular times may be better than others if you have a special interest within the hobby. For instance, for song spring and early summer is clearly the best time of year, birdsong being at its height during the months of April, May and June. This is also the season when the bird's plumage is at the brightest to attract a mate. Many of our migrants return from places like Africa; and there are all the activities connected with breeding and nesting. The weather, too, is likely to be at its best at this time of year!

Among the attractions of winter birdwatching are the visitors flying in from the severer climates of the Arctic, Norway, Sweden and Eastern Europe. Fieldfares, redwing, brambling (a close relative of the chaffinch) are only to be seen here during that time of year. A good habitat for

17

Robin

winter birdwatching is the seashore, though here you will have to be aware of the state of the tide. When the tide is out, the birds will be searching for food in the sand and mud flats, and may well be a long way from you. One complication of pursuing the hobby in winter is that many books on birds only illustrate them in summer plumage. In fact a bird's plumage can change considerably over the year; it is far less bright, for instance, when nesting is over. Between summer and winter there may be a transitional phase unportrayed in any book at all. The way to overcome this difficulty is to learn to identify the birds by their shape, the way they fly and by the other features mentioned earlier.

Although most birds tend to fall silent during the winter months you will still be able to hear the robin. Maybe this is why he appears on so many of our Christmas cards. I have often heard them singing defiantly at each other in winter. Arthur tells me that they are doing so to mark the boundaries of their territory.

The best time of day for this hobby is early morning. Few humans will yet have been around to disturb the birds and, particularly in spring, the most beautiful songs are to be heard as the birds wake from their night's sleep. One of the earliest to contribute to the dawn chorus is the blackbird which sometimes starts to sing about forty minutes before sunrise; he will soon be joined by others until they are all in that beautiful full song that wakes me early and enchants me as I lie half asleep, half awake listening. It sounds as though they are singing joyously; in fact they are very purposeful – telling females of the species that they want a mate, or defining and defending their territory. 'Keep off,' they say, 'this is my patch.'

Whereas this is one purpose of a bird's song, it may also have a variety of other calls that can be used to communicate a great variety of messages. Arthur told me some details of this while we sat and drank coffee in the hide. A bird's call indicates what species it is, and subtle variations also show the bird's particular identity, just as human voices are distinguishable from each other. A fascinating point is that birds of the same species sing slightly differently over different parts of the country, rather as we have regional dialects. Calls are used to warn of the approach of danger, and maybe you have heard a blackbird indicating the presence of a cat. Usually it is the male bird that sings, one aim being, as I have said, to attract a mate. Some birds achieve the same effect by displaying distinctive plumage, such as the bright red breast of the cock robin and the peacock's brilliant fan. So it is not surprising that it is often the birds with the less conspicuous plumage that will sing best.

The period of birdsong is fairly short, singing becoming more subdued and less frequent as summer approaches. An exception to this short period is the mistle thrush. Whereas most birds do not sing in bad weather (have you noticed that the dawn chorus starts late on an overcast, miserable morning?) the mistle thrush gets under way in January undeterred by anything except perhaps heavy snow. It will even sing in a thunderstorm – hence its nickname, 'Storm Cock'.

After the initial burst of early morning song, birds cease to sing as a choir for the rest of the day, though they do still sing as individuals intermittently. They can still be watched, of course, though it is as well to remember that in warm weather they are least active between about noon and two, the hottest time of the day. Birds sing again in the evening before settling down for the night, but less exuberantly than in the morning. The evening also holds other attractions for birdwatchers: owls fly in the dusk, in winter geese come back to roost from the fields where they have spent the day, and you may well see ducks as they head off for a night's feeding in ditches and ponds.

## Habitats

To some extent your experience of birdwatching will be determined by where you live and how often you are able to go out. But as I said earlier every type of countryside – and town – is inhabited by birds. Indeed, over the years many species have learned to adapt to changes in the environment. There have been losses as our cities have eaten farther and farther into the countryside; but on the other hand, over the last few years the nest-boxes, food and protection provided in towns have attracted many species back into built-up areas.

A new habitat has been created by the motorways. Although they devour great tracts of land their wide banks are becoming natural nature reserves. The banks are rarely disturbed, the grass is never cut, and no poisonous chemicals are sprayed on them. Many small mammals and birds are attracted to these and soon get used to the traffic; they are quickly followed by predators, and so it is unlikely that you will travel for too many miles along a motorway without seeing a kestrel hovering overhead.

Hen kestrel

On the bad side, however, are the continuing losses of hedgerows and trees, the natural nesting-places and refuges of so many species. Britain's farming is now perhaps the most highly mechanised in the world, and many hedges have been cut down as farmers have enlarged their fields to make the most of the new machinery. Many trees have gone, lost through felling or disease. In addition to this the use of pesticides on crops has had a disastrous effect on some species. Other types of habitat have also been altered by man. The reclamation of marshland has harmed the populations of ducks, geese and the waders that probe with their long bills to seek food in the shallow water and mud. What were once wild, lonely stretches of coast are now occupied by caravan sites or estates, and seabirds such as the ringed plover and terns have found it impossible to cope with holiday-makers trampling unknowingly over their nests on the sand and shingle.

In the second section of this book Arthur Gilpin describes the fifty or so British birds that you are most likely to see. Here I will suggest some of the habitats in which you may like to watch.

As I live in a big city and am most familiar with those birds, I will start there. I have already mentioned some of the birds that are to be found commonly. You will find a lot to note even about house sparrows, those lively, chirpy birds that always seem to be busy. Sparrows often nest in cracks and holes in buildings and I have some noisily building a nest in

Cock house sparrow

Young mallard

the wall just below my kitchen window at this moment. Have you ever thought why a pair of birds chooses a particular site for a nest? Gilbert White believed that early in the year sparrows chose nesting-places in buildings, but then raised a second brood in more open, cooler places in the summer. Perhaps by observing the birds carefully you could tell whether or not he was correct.

A slightly wider range of birds is to be found in parks and gardens, and I have already suggested how you can attract them by putting out food, water and nest-boxes. In a garden you may be fortunate enough to get to know your birds as individuals, watching a pair raise a brood, following the progress of the fledgelings and recording their behaviour over a period of years. This sort of activity does enable you to take a very personal involvement in the hobby.

Many public parks have ponds and lakes, the habitat of a great variety of duck and water birds that often accept food from the hand. If you leave the town and go to wider stretches of inland water you may be rewarded by sights of rare visitors. This is the time when a good fieldguide and clear observation will be essential.

The seaside is a wonderful place for birdwatching. The range of species varies with the type of land – whether it is river estuary, marsh, shore or cliff. The symbol of the RSPB is a coastal bird – the avocet, and its story is one of the successes of modern conservation. Several hundred years ago the striking black-and-white plumage, long blue legs and sweeping, upturning bill of this species was a common sight near the Suffolk coast. Drainage of the fenlands coupled with the fact that the avocet's eggs were prized for food and its plumage for fishing flies, meant that by the beginning of this century they were no longer to be found breeding in this country. But after the last war they again came back, began to breed, were protected and are now welcome summer visitors.

Cliffs and rocky islands are popular haunts of seabirds nesting so closely

Edge of the marsh

Shelduck in flight and oystercatchers on the shore in winter

Guillemots crowded on to pinnacles at the Farne Islands

and precariously that you wonder how they manage to stay put. My greatest chance to see birds like this was off the north-east coast of England when I was filming at the Farne Islands. We took our small boat in quite close along the edge of several islands that were uninhabited except for myriads of birds. I was particularly taken with the puffins with their brightly coloured beaks, easy to spot as they darted over the waves. One of the best cliffs to look at seabirds in Britain is at Bempton in Yorkshire. Here you can see about nine different species, all vying for a nesting-place on the narrow ledges, and this is the only part of the mainland where you can find Britain's largest seabird, the gannet, nesting.

Back inland, rivers are a great habitat for wildlife. The banks are often lined by trees and bushes; fish may be found in the water and flies skim the surface. So here are food and cover for many birds including the heron standing patiently on one long leg, the other tucked underneath him. At the sight of a fish or eel the bird stabs down with incredible speed to seize its prey. Another bird I love to watch by rivers is the kingfisher, a brilliant blue splash of colour darting swiftly by in search of fish.

Less flamboyant, perhaps, are the birds of the heathland, such as the meadow pipit. One well-known inhabitant of this sort of region is the cuckoo which, as you will know, is the only British bird to lay its eggs in other birds' nests. Heathland is characterised by soils that are too poor to support much farming. You will often find bracken, gorse or pines in this sort of country. Another characteristic is that the soil will be dry.

In the north and west of Britain are the higher moors and mountains which are often wet and in winter experience extremes of cold and snow. This is the country for game birds such as grouse and ptarmigan and for birds of prey. The most magnificent of the latter is perhaps the golden eagle which Arthur tells me is reasonably common in some parts of Scotland. During a fortnight's trip there he saw them every day from the main road, and one morning while driving his car he saw a whole family of golden eagles.

Each type of land, then, favours its own particular species of birds. Out in the fields you may hear the peewit, named for his call 'p'weet, p'weet', and there is also that marvellous songster, the skylark, which always

A red-throated diver on its loch in north-west Scotland

26

makes me think of hot summer days. Hovering up so high you can hardly see them without binoculars, they warble away prettily. Not that they only sing in the heat of summer: I have been cheered by the song of this little bird early on a March morning when I have been out horse-riding in Richmond Park. Lastly, do not forget the woodlands, which again have their distinctive bird species, whether it is woodpeckers among the deciduous trees or the turkey-sized capercaillie in the Scottish pine forests. Tits, siskins and our tiniest British bird, the goldcrest, are some of the other species hidden deep in the cool, dark, quiet pinewoods.

## Going on with the hobby

I hope I have indicated some of the potential range of your birdwatching. There are many ways in which you can take the hobby further. You may go on to become one of those 'twitchers' who try to see how many different species they can record. In this country about five hundred species are listed, over half of them living here all the year round, and the others coming as visitors in summer or winter.

Another development of your birdwatching will be your ability to understand bird behaviour; you will to some measure become a scientist. Perhaps you will have a chance to involve yourself, for instance, in the fascinating theories that surround the subject of migration. Since the beginning of this century ornithologists have been ringing visiting birds to find out where they come from and where they go. Birds have much to face on these transcontinental journeys – starvation, storms and attacks by predators including man. Sometimes there are more unexpected hazards: the common whitethroat, for instance, winters south of the Sahara. For many years its chances of survival were damaged by the desert extending a hundred miles farther south after a change in climate. Luckily the species seems to have adjusted itself.

The main motive for migration is food. What is so intriguing is that the migrations are quite instinctive. Often parent birds will migrate before their young, yet when it is time the young bird, who has never made the journey before, knows exactly where to go. In a few cases, some members of a particular species move on while others do not. The meadow pipit is a classic example. Some breed here and stay all year round, some move south into France for the winter and yet others that breed in northern and eastern Europe come and spend their winters in Britain. Usually, our summer visitors set off for the Mediterranean and parts of Africa, where they enjoy the warmth and sunshine while we are having our winter. From northern Europe and the Arctic where the winters are much more

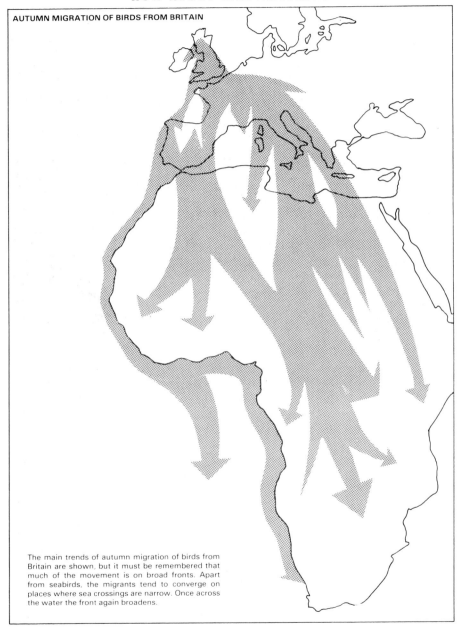

AUTUMN MIGRATION OF BIRDS FROM BRITAIN

The main trends of autumn migration of birds from Britain are shown, but it must be remembered that much of the movement is on broad fronts. Apart from seabirds, the migrants tend to converge on places where sea crossings are narrow. Once across the water the front again broadens.

The hide made of odds and ends from which the robin on page 18 was photographed

severe, birds will come to Britain for its milder climate. When they return the male bird often arrives a few days before the female, so he can stake out his territory without which he has little hope of attracting a mate.

Migration is certainly a complex story. How do birds navigate those vast distances? One theory is that they use the sun and the stars, and that this is sufficient for them to return not only to the same locality, but to the very same site. You could perhaps help provide information that would clarify some of the difficulties. Eventually you may be allowed a licence to trap and ring birds as part of a proper census.

Another area in which there is so much still to learn is that of one bird's behaviour towards another. I have mentioned that you could try and work out why a sparrow chooses a particular site for its nest, or you could try and come to know birds as individuals. Gradually you may come to understand more about courtship, display, aggression and all the other interesting aspects of behaviour. Photography would be a useful aid here, and in any case photography is one of the most satisfying pursuits connected with the hobby. As you become more enthusiastic and knowledge-

29

able you will be able to share your information with clubs and chosen colleagues; you will become part of a select community of people whose interest has developed and deepened. Photography is an extension of this. Arthur Gilpin's patience and skill have produced results which everyone – not just keen ornithologists – enjoys; his hobby has given a vast amount of pleasure to other people. Photography can become expensive if you go on to use special lenses and equipment, but on the other hand, as Arthur has demonstrated in his beautiful book, *Nature Photography*, there are many ways of limiting the cost.

Another extension of the activity is recording birdsong, and, of course, you may decide that making recordings is what gives you the greatest pleasure, whether they are of birds or animals. Again, equipment can be expensive, though quite good results can be achieved if you use your limited resources to their best advantage.

Well, as I learned during my day with Arthur Gilpin, there is certainly a fascinating range of activities combined under the general heading of 'birdwatching'. The study of birds is a huge, varied subject with interests to suit all sorts of people, wherever they live. Remember the 'Birdman of Alcatraz', the prisoner who became a world authority on birds from his own cell before you say to yourself, 'There's nothing for me to see here.'

As Arthur writes on page 95, there is a society catering specially for the young birdwatcher who wishes to extend his or her knowledge. This is the Young Ornithologists Club, which is part of the Royal Society for the Protection of Birds. Why not join? It could be fun. I am sure that this is a hobby that will give you many years of pleasure and enjoyment.

## Remember that ...

● It is illegal to kill most species of birds at any time of the year, or to take their eggs or young.

● If you go looking for nests, even if you don't take the eggs, you will tread down undergrowth and break branches. That disturbance can lead boys or animals that do take eggs to the nests you find.

● It is illegal to disturb any species on Schedule 1 of the Protection of Birds Acts at the nest, for any reason whatever.

● Young birds are usually not lost until they are found. Their parents know where they are, but if you find them and carry them away they have less chance of survival.

● Should you see a fluffy looking young tawny owl in a bush or on the ground, **do not touch it**. In addition to what is written above, it can be dangerous to do so. Parent tawny owls sometimes attack those handling their young. I know of several cases where people have required stitches in the wounds inflicted and a friend of mine lost an eye in such an encounter. In any case young tawnys are deceptive. Beneath a covering of down they often have enough feathers for them to fly and do not require any assistance.

● When in the country do not break down walls or fences, leave gates open or light fires that can get out of control.

● You should ask permission before going on private land.

● When you are in a nature or bird reserve you are expected to observe the rules, whether a warden is with you or not.

● Wet ground and sand can be unpredictable, so don't go unescorted on to marshes or unknown shores. When crossing saltings or reed-beds, do not jump ditches unless you are sure the ground at the other side will bear your weight.

● Almost every spring young people die from falling off cliffs or are drowned; take care and don't be one of them.

# 2  THE PRACTICAL ASPECTS
## *by Arthur Gilpin*

### Techniques and equipment

One reason why birdwatching is so popular is that it is possible to enjoy the hobby without spending a lot of money. For young people this is a great advantage. When I was thirteen I played rugby and cricket on Saturdays, but Sundays and holidays were spent wandering along country lanes and footpaths. My country walks were not just aimed at getting me from one place to another, so I did not rush along, but moved slowly taking note of the birds. If you run through a farmyard, the hens, ducks and geese scurry away in alarm. There is no reason to expect wild birds to act differently. As Val has mentioned I had no binoculars in those days, but my eyes and ears were good. When I heard a birdsong that I did not know coming from some bush or hedge, I endeavoured to see the songster. I would sit down and wait for the singer to emerge from cover. In that way I learned which bird sang which song. When the trees were clothed in leaves I would then know what birds were around me, even if I could not see them.

Besides waiting for birds I stalked them, using any available cover to hide my approach. Like most boys of my generation I had read *The Last of the Mohicans* and I tried to copy the hunting methods of the Red Indians that were described in it, but my aim was to see, not to kill. I shall never forget the excitement of moving as quietly as I could through a wood by a mill dam and after crawling up the bank, seeing my first drake teal at close quarters. Peering between clumps of rushes and keeping my head as low as possible, I was able to see the bird's dark eye and the feathers of metallic green surrounding it. I made a sketch of the head in my notebook and when I compared it with the pictures in a bird book, I found that only teal had such markings.

Later I built hides at places where I knew birds would be. At one pond where waterfowl gathered I got permission to build two. On a place by the edge of it there were some overhanging willows. With some slender branches and cord, I built the framework of a screen beneath them. To fill the gaps in this I wove in the stems and leaves of bulrushes. By the way, that plant is also known to botanists as reedmace. The hide at the other side of the lake was an igloo of stones, with dead branches used to span the top.

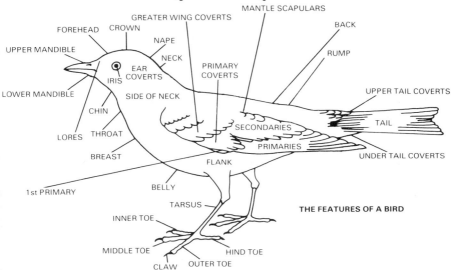

THE FEATURES OF A BIRD

In both cases I built at a place which I could approach unseen by any birds on the water. If the birds are disturbed as you enter a hide, they may stay away a long time; therefore, before siting a hide, the way to it must be planned.

Of course houses act as hides from which you can watch birds in gardens. If yours is a large garden you may wish to build a tree-house of scrap material and watch from there.

From hides you can watch birds that come to drink at ponds, as well as those that swim on the water. You can watch waders on the shore, as they are brought closer to you by the advancing tide. In that case you must make sure the hide is above the reach of a full tide. Also you can build a hide in a suitable place and tempt birds to it by putting out food. Pigeons and finches come to corn spread on the ground and tits come to nuts or fat hung from a tree. Many species can be attracted to quite small gardens if suitable food is provided.

There are many advantages in working from a hide. As you are invisible to the birds they will come close; for once they are used to the hide they will ignore it. That is, of course, if you do not make a noise or poke out arms or binoculars. Also you can sit and write your notes in moderate comfort. Large hides are to be found in some of the nature and bird

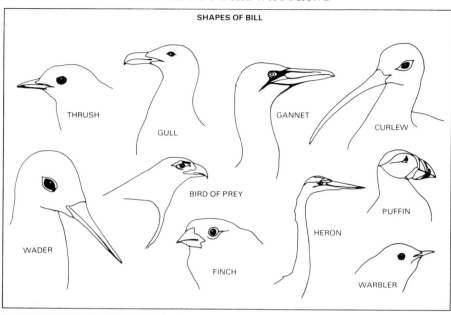

**SHAPES OF BILL**

THRUSH

GULL

GANNET

CURLEW

WADER

BIRD OF PREY

FINCH

HERON

PUFFIN

WARBLER

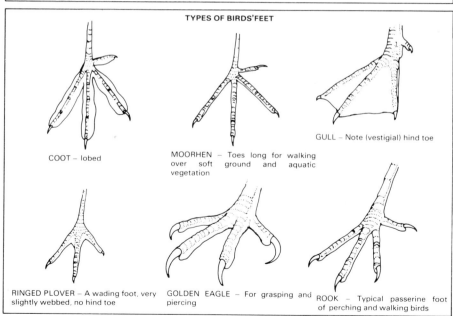

**TYPES OF BIRDS'FEET**

COOT – lobed

MOORHEN – Toes long for walking over soft ground and aquatic vegetation

GULL – Note (vestigial) hind toe

RINGED PLOVER – A wading foot, very slightly webbed, no hind toe

GOLDEN EAGLE – For grasping and piercing

ROOK – Typical passerine foot of perching and walking birds

reserves that are listed at the end of this book. These accommodate several people and are watertight. Even in pouring rain, Val and I saw plenty of birds from one of them when we birdwatched together.

On page 29 there is a picture of a hide I made of odds and ends. It was situated in a disused corner of a garden. The photographs of house sparrow and robin, on pages 21 and 18, were taken from it.

The use of a notebook in the field is a great help. Not only can you record the details of the birds you are seeing for the first time, but you can keep lists of birds seen and notes on their behaviour. Write your notes and descriptions as neatly as possible and try to have a standard system for both. When noting the particulars of a new bird you will require to know the names of its parts and feather groups. The illustration on page 33 will assist you. Having read Val's comments on note taking and looked at the illustrations of bills and feet on page 34, you should be able to get good descriptive notes. Upon returning home these can be compared with pictures of birds in books. When I was young those used were borrowed from the public library and usually had two or more volumes in order to include all the British birds. Now there are much more compact books called fieldguides. They have coloured pictures of all the birds you are likely to see. As they can be carried in the pocket, it is possible, when you have the guide with you in the field, to identify the bird by comparing it with the illustrations. You may not be able to afford a fieldguide at first and it is then that your notebook will be most useful. It will still be required even after you have bought a suitable fieldguide. There will be times when you see something new and do not have the guide with you. In addition, you will wish to record your excursions and in later years your notebooks will enable you to refresh your memories of birds and places.

Many birdwatchers have larger books at home in which, using their field notes as a basis, they write fuller descriptions of birds and of their outings. Others transfer their notes to a card index system. For this purpose the cards should be reasonably large, 5 in × 3 in (13 cm × 8 cm) being about right, but there is no reason why they should not be larger if you wish.

Val mentions the expense of binoculars, and normally they cost more than any other item bought to increase your enjoyment of birdwatching. Even so, in real value they are cheaper now than they were forty years ago. Your family may already have some or you may get binoculars for a birthday or Christmas present. Perhaps your parents, uncle or aunt should read what follows. The great advantage of having binoculars is that through them the bird looks much nearer; ten times if you are using 10× binoculars and eight times if 8× are used. That is what the first figure engraved on the binocular means. The figure after the cross may be 30, 40 or 50; that is the diameter in millimetres of each of the front lenses. All other things being equal the larger that number the more the light reaching the eye.

However the amount of light to reach the eye is also affected by the magnification, that is the first number. One can get a guide to this by dividing the second of the numbers by the first. For instance if the numbers are 8 × 32, 8 × 40 or 10 × 50 the simple division below indicates the proportion of light:

$$32 \div 8 \text{ gives the power of } 4$$
$$40 \div 8 \quad ,, \quad ,, \quad ,, \quad ,, \ 5$$
$$50 \div 10 \quad ,, \quad ,, \quad ,, \quad ,, \ 5$$

You will see that 8 × 32 produce a power of 4 and both 8 × 40 and 10 × 50 give 5. The first have a bright enough image in average daylight, but are less satisfactory in very dull conditions. Giving a brighter image than the first the other two can be used well into the dusk. There are other sizes of glasses, but most birdwatchers use glasses close to these magnifications. Although 8 × 30 – a very popular size – allows a little less light through than the 32, the difference is too slight to be noticed.

It may seem that the binoculars with the biggest magnification and largest front lenses are the best for birdwatching, but there are other things to consider. In the first place such a glass would be very heavy (there may be exceptions but they are expensive). Secondly, the bigger the magnification the more difficult it is to hold the glass steady. Also the depth of field – that is the distance between the nearest and the farthest object in focus – is less with the larger glass. That means it is necessary to refocus more often on a bird moving away from or towards the observer. In addition, the field of view – the area seen through the binocular – is smaller with a ten times binocular than one of eight times magnification.

For a person with a steady hand, the ten times binocular is an excellent instrument for working in wide open spaces such as moorland, lake or estuary. The birds are likely to be a long way from the observer and the extra magnification is valuable. In woodland, particularly with small birds, because of its greater depth and more extensive field of view the eight times scores. For young people I recommend 8 × 30 binoculars. They are small in bulk and weight, can be focused quickly and, partly because they are the most popular size, tend to be the cheapest. If as you grow older you feel the need for higher power, they can still be retained. for woodland work and a telescope obtained for observation on estuary and moorland.

## Fieldguides

Bird fieldguides follow a general principle of showing coloured pictures of the birds, with significant identification features indicated. Where the male and female of a species differ in appearance, both are usually depicted. It is normal to show the bird in the plumage it has when in this country. In the case of species that are with us at all times of the year, if their appearance changes with the seasons, both summer and winter plumage may be shown. Where the guides do differ is in the areas they deal with, the way the information is presented and the amount of descriptive matter they contain. That means that before you buy a guide you should give considerable thought to deciding exactly what you require.

For instance, although it is nice to have all the species in Europe in one guide, you could find that at first such a large number of them is confusing. The families of birds are, for scientific reasons, listed in a standard order. Because I know that order, I find it most convenient to use a fieldguide in which it is used. That is true of most experienced birdwatchers and some of them have made fun of a guide that lists the species in relation to habitat and size. But in my classes for beginners, I have found that many find that guide the most useful.

In the brief list of fieldguides that follows, I have not included any that are too large to carry comfortably. If price is important you will find that some can be had in either hard covers or a cheaper soft-back edition.

As the *R.S.P.B. Guide to Birds*, written by David Saunders and published by Hamlyn, deals only with the commoner birds, it is not as thick as some of the others. It is also less expensive than most. The birds are described family by family. The description and other information about each species is on the page opposite its portrait. That is a great help as both can be taken in at a glance. The coloured plates of the birds are good, although one or two have a yellow cast. There are some very useful sketches of birds in flight. These are on coloured leaves that are easy to find. As birds often show a distinctive pattern when flying, they are most helpful. So is the map showing all the R.S.P.B. Reserves. This book is good value and will not confuse the beginner with an over-abundance of species.

*The Pocket Guide to British Birds*, written by R. S. R. Fitter and published

Gulls following the plough: these are mostly black-headed gulls in winter plumage

by Collins, is arranged in order of habitat and size. If one sees a large bird on a lake one first finds the section for Water Birds. The bird will then come under the heading Long. All the pictures are in the middle of the book and apart from those of black and white birds they are coloured. Many of them are of flying birds and there are also useful pictures of juvenile and intermediate plumages. In order to give an idea of the scale of the pictures there is, in the corner of each plate, a silhouette of a house sparrow. The publishers point out that on a few plates the size of the sparrow is not exactly right. In no case is the scale so far out that it seriously affects the comparisons. What can be slightly trying is finding the information that is in a different part of the book to the picture.

*A Field Guide to the Birds of Britain and Europe,* authors Roger Peterson, Guy Mountford and P. A. D. Hollom, published by Collins, and *The Hamlyn Guide to the Birds of Britain and Europe,* written by Bertel Brun, obviously cover the same area. Both list the species in scientific order and use small maps to show the European distribution of each species. The main difference is that although there is a brief comment opposite the picture of the bird in Collins' book, the main information may be many pages from it; whereas in the Hamlyn version both picture and descriptive matter are together. Both are very good and used by a large number of birdwatchers.

On the day the publisher required this manuscript, I saw a new edition of *The Oxford Book of Birds*. It is smaller and more pocketable than most of the fieldguides. First published in a larger format by the Oxford University Press as a general-purpose bird book, it contains information on more facets of bird life than the normal guides. It is written by Bruce Cambell and illustrated by Donald Watson. The birds are shown in their normal habitats and the information is on the page opposite the plate. To keep in all the information that there was in the original, the size of print is small, but not difficult to read. This book should fulfil all a young birdwatcher's requirements for several years.

There are several other fieldguides and also large numbers of small, reasonably priced identification books, that deal either with groups of birds or those to be found in certain habitats. Many are good, but some are not. If you are in doubt, try to find an older person with some knowledge of birds to advise you.

In addition to books there are wallcharts showing many different species of birds. These can be used to decorate your room, and from seeing them frequently, you will begin to remember the characteristics of the individual birds. The charts produced by the R.S.P.B. are very good. If you live in a town it is likely that once a year there will be a show of films produced by that Society. When that happens there will also be a sales counter at which charts and many other birdy things may be bought. If you cannot obtain them that way, they can be ordered by post from the R.S.P.B., The Lodge, Sandy, Bedfordshire SG19 2DL.

## Other books

I have already mentioned that the books I used at home when I was a boy were borrowed from the local lending library. Until you can afford text-books you will do well to follow that example. You will find there are many advantages. Firstly you will be able to discover the information you seek and secondly you will be able to read more books than you could afford to buy. Reading a variety of books will not only broaden your knowledge of birds, but it will also help you to decide on the books you wish to own and save you from wasting money on others. Home reading can be in search of either information or for pleasure. Fortunately there are plenty of bird books that provide both.

Fieldguides are primarily for identification purposes and the need to

▲ Deciduous woodland

▼ Coniferous woodland

keep them pocketable restricts the amount of information they can contain. Therefore if you wish to know in more detail the way a bird lives, you will require to find the information in books you can read at leisure.

The five-volume *Handbook of British Birds* published by H. F. & G. Wetherby is the standard work for those interested in birds. In it is the accumulated knowledge of a large number of ornithologists. Each species and its habits are dealt with in far greater detail than one finds in a fieldguide. There is a feather-by-feather description of each species in all its plumages, from nestling to adult and throughout the year. Unfortunately this book is now out of print and secondhand sets fetch high prices. Also a lot of new information has been obtained since it was published. To deal with the requirement of a more up-to-date book dealing with a wider area, the first volume of *Birds of Europe, the Middle East and North Africa* has now been released by Oxford University Press. The rest of the volumes will be published annually over the next eight years. This is also expensive and it is very unlikely that you will be able to borrow either of these books from the library, although you may be allowed to consult them in the reference sections of some.

However, one book in which you will find the answers to many of your questions is the *Readers Digest/AA Book of British Birds*. In it you can read of the ancestry of birds, their history in these islands, their migrations, their sight and hearing, where to see birds and many more things. Although it is too large and heavy to carry on country walks, if you are doing your birdwatching from your window or a car, it can also be used as a fieldguide. It contains coloured field identification pictures and portraits of the birds, as well as descriptions of them. They are arranged in habitats.

The first bird book I owned was *The Birds of the British Isles* by T. A. Coward, published by Warnes. It has recently been revised and more up-to-date photographs are included. Highly readable, it has a coloured picture of each of the species described. I still refer to it on occasion.

What you read for pleasure will depend on your own taste, but I don't think any boy or girl would fail to enjoy Henry Williamson's books. Two of the best for young birdwatchers are *The Lone Swallows* and *The Peregrine's Saga*. These have been reprinted several times and could well be obtainable at your library. If not, it is possible that the librarian would get them on loan from another, if your parents requested him to do so.

There have been very large numbers of books written about birds. Some are on one species, others on behaviour, or about birding expeditions and most counties have books on the birds found in them. You have a wide choice.

# 3 AIDS TO THE HOBBY
## *by Arthur Gilpin*

### Identification

The more you know about birds the more species you will recognise. For instance, it is a great help to know when the birds are in this country. Then you require to know where to look for each species (its habitat). Finally, knowing something of its behaviour and movements will assist in identifying it.

Birds make calls of various sorts. These range from alarm notes to song. Descriptions in words can only be a rough guide, but there are many useful records and tapes of bird calls now available. If you know the type of food a species feeds upon you have a further indication of where to look for it. As some birds change their feeding habits in winter their habitat may also change. One must then look for them in a different place. Some birds gather in spectacular flocks to roost, others sleep singly and some prepare a roosting place.

In the descriptions that follow there will be information on all these things. With a book of this size there will not be room to include all the British birds, but it is my intention to give information about the birds you are most likely to see. In cases where we have several reasonably common species of one family, the one you are most likely to know is chosen and the others compared to it. Textbooks on birds present the families in a standard order, but in this book we have attempted to start with those species most of you will see first. The meaning of the symbols is as shown below.

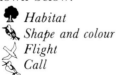

*Habitat*
*Shape and colour*
*Flight*
*Call*

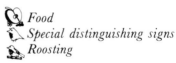

*Food*
*Special distinguishing signs*
*Roosting*

### House Sparrow

Even in the hearts of great cities you will find house sparrows. Although at one time a European species, they have now spread to many places, including America and South Africa. The spread commenced in the last century, with the increase of shipping.

It was not until the Clean Air Acts were introduced that it was possible in cities to see what this bird's plumage was like. Owing to the dirty atmosphere begriming their feathers, they looked drab-grey creatures. The cock sparrow is a handsome bird. Some $5\frac{3}{4}$ inches (14·5 cm) long he has a slatey crown, black bib and a brown back streaked with black. The cheeks and underparts are pale grey. There is less variation in the plumage of the hen and the young in their first feathers. They lack the grey crown and black throat and are a duller shade of brown.

When feeding on the ground house sparrows hop. Their diet is very varied, ranging from household scraps to seeds and insects.

Although its normal note is a penetrating chirp, the house sparrow has quite a vocubulary, as you will realise when you hear them quarrel in the gutter. At night they retire to holes in buildings.

## Robin

A bird that is to be seen at all seasons, the robin holds a strong position in the affection of British people. When Britons have settled in some distant land, they have often named a red-breasted bird Robin.

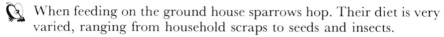

In spring and summer it is a bird of woodland rides, hedgerows and copses. When the leaves change colour in the autumn, many come close to the habitations of man and stay there throughout the winter. Then, this bird's well-rounded shape is a common sight in gardens, orchards and farmyards.

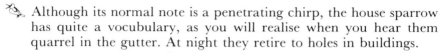

About the same size as a house sparrow, but more plump, its orange-red breast is the robin's most noticeable feature. The upper parts are plain olive-brown and the belly white. Cock and hen are alike, but young birds in their first plumage lack the orange-red, being generally brown and much spotted.

Feeding on the ground the robin hops quite quickly. A characteristic habit is for the bird to dash from cover, collect an item of food, then return to shelter. Apart from the food put out by householders, this bird's diet is mainly of insects and worms.

The rather rambling song of the robin has in it many rich notes. It is sung in spring and autumn, but in the later part of the year it seems to lack the fire of the mating song. When angry the robin makes a sharp 'tic, tic' scolding note.

Although it roosts singly in bushes, it may also be found doing so in buildings.

## Dunnock or Hedge Sparrow

Much more unobtrusive than the last described species the dunnock is resident with us. It is not a close relative of the house sparrow and I prefer the name dunnock.

Its habitat varies from gardens and hedgerows to open woodlands with plenty of undergrowth.

With a rather dark brown crown, cheeks and back, and grey on the rest of the body, the dunnock is not a bird to attract attention. It has the noticeably slender bill of an insect feeder.

On the ground it either hops, or walks in a crouching way. One very characteristic action is the very sharp flick and readjustment of the wings. The movement is rather like a man trying to settle a badly fitting jacket. One of its vernacular names is 'shufflewing'.

When there are plenty of insects available it feeds on them, but in winter it exists mainly on seeds. Hard winters affect it less than might be expected and it seems to find food where a robin cannot.

A sweet warble of short duration, the song of the dunnock is pleasant without being striking. Often the presence of this bird is betrayed by the rather shrill 'tseep' call it frequently makes. In winter I have come across groups of four or five of them and the calls were almost continuous.

## Wren

This is another common bird that does not leave this country in winter.

Few British birds can have a more varied habitat than the wren. I have come across this species on mountains, sea-cliffs, commons, in woodlands and public parks.

Its small size, closely barred, brown plumage and cocked tail make this an easily recognised bird.

One has only to watch this bird feeding to realise that the scientific name of 'Troglodytes' – meaning cave dweller – is well deserved. With quick, rather jerky movements it enters cavities and overhangs of banks, as well as working its way through root tangles in its search. It is in such places that it finds the insects, spiders and cocoons that it feeds upon.

44

Wren

 There is a rattling quality about the notes and song of the wren, the latter sounds loud and aggressive for such a small bird.

 Several wrens will roost together. One winter's evening I watched eight go into one of their old nests in a farm outbuilding.

## Starling

Although many starlings that nest here do not leave the country, the large flocks seen in winter – mainly at roosting places – are generally of Continental birds.

This is a most adaptable species and one finds it in most places from sea-cliff to moorland.

In winter the dark glossy plumage of the starling is very speckled. That is because some of the back feathers are tipped with pale buff, and some on the underparts with white. As spring approaches those tips wear off, leaving an almost unspotted dark plumage shot with purple and green.

Running quickly it stops from time to time to probe the ground, sometimes opening its bill after it has been inserted.

Various grubs, insects and worms are taken and in autumn so are fruits.

In many large cities where starlings sleep on the ledges of buildings, the winter roosts are spectacular, but in the country they can be even more so. One evening, motoring inland after visiting the coast, I saw a huge black cloud in the sky in front of me. Three miles

Starling feeding on seed in winter

46

farther on I realised it was made up of starlings. I continued and the trees by the roadside soon had almost as many birds in them as they had leaves in summer. Stopping by a field where the birds covered the ground, I went in. The nearest birds took off and progressively so did the others. It was as if a large black carpet had been lifted up from one corner. This was only one of several gathering places for starlings going to roost in a wood some distance away. It was estimated that there were 3,000,000 immigrants birds in the actual roost.

At the same time, birds of this species that had bred here were going to roost singly and in pairs, using hollow trees and cavities under house roofs in nearby villages; there they had slept all year. Even when the large roosts were close they showed no inclination to join them.

### Treecreeper

At all times of the year you may see this bird searching the bark of trees for food. It is to be found in woodlands and parks, both private and public.

 Small, only five inches (12·5 cm) long and a third of that being the tail, the treecreeper's upper plumage is brown, spotted and streaked with pale buff and near white. Both the under-parts and the streaks above the eyes are white. Its bill is longish, slender and down-curved.

 Usually its method of collecting food is to start at the foot of a tree and, searching the crevices of the bark as it goes, climb upwards. Reaching a considerable height it will drop off, fly to the base of another tree and repeat the operation. It is likely that you will first spot the treecreeper as it makes one of the descending flights. When climbing with tail pressed against the tree, its plumage blends with the bark.

Spiders, their cocoons, insects and their larvae are the staple food of this species.

 Its voice is high-pitched and its song is in two short phrases with a noticeable stop between.

Treecreeper

Where there are those large redwood trees known as Wellingtonias, treecreepers will excavate roosting places in their thick, friable bark. These are about the shape and size of half a table tennis ball. Otherwise treecreepers sleep in natural cavities or behind loose bark.

## Nuthatch

At any time of the year you may hear, in England, the clear whistle of the nuthatch.

Its habitat is very similar to the last described species, but it climbs on walls more often.

Nuthatch

A short stumpy bird with strong bill and feet, this is the only species we have that moves up, down and across tree trunks with equal ease. Unlike the treecreeper and woodpecker it does not use its stumpy tail as a support when climbing. Its feathers are blue-grey on the top of the body. There is a black mark through the eye and the underbody is buff, except for the flanks which are chestnut coloured. At each side of the tip of the tail is a small white patch.

Nuthatches move about the trunks of trees with quick jumps.

The fruits, seeds and nuts of trees are part of its food, but it does also take insects and their larvae, etc. Nuts are sometimes wedged in cracks, in order that the nuthatch can hammer them open with its powerful bill.

This species roosts in holes in trees and sometimes in crevices in buildings.

## Kingfisher

The kingfisher, about the most brilliantly coloured of our birds, remains here the winter through. In normal years it can catch the small fish, etc., that it feeds upon throughout the whole twelve months. But in very cold winters, like that of 1962–3 when many streams froze over, large numbers can perish.

The haunt of this bird is by the sides of streams and rivers. Less frequently they are to be seen by lakes and sometimes I have seen them at large reservoirs.

With a short, stubby tail, long bill, back coloured in brilliant blue that shades to green in some lightings and bright chestnut below, the sparrow-sized kingfisher is unlike any other British bird.

Its flight is swift and direct, usually it is low as the bird follows the twists and turns of river and stream. When crossing large lakes or land I have seen it flying at considerable heights. Its normal manner of obtaining food is to watch from some perch overhanging water and plunge down upon its prey. Then the fish or tadpole is carried back to the perch to be swallowed. At other times it will hover on fast-beating wings and dive from flight.

The approach of a kingfisher is often heralded by a loud clear pipe that is frequently repeated.

Kingfisher

*Heron*

At all seasons you may expect to see the rather gaunt, grey shape of the heron at the waterside.

It feeds by rivers, streams, lakes and in marshes. In hard weather it visits the seashore.

This is one of the largest birds you will see in the British country-side, measuring about a yard (90 cm) from the tip of its beak to the end of its tail. Its bill, neck and legs are long. Except for the black main flight feathers (primaries) the upper sides of the wings and back are grey. There is a line of black down the front of the throat and from each eye, the feathers in the latter forming a plume down the back of the head. The under-parts are pale grey, while the bill and legs are yellow.

In flight with its head resting between its shoulders, legs out-stretched and with large, broad wings, the heron has a distinctive silhouette. When feeding in the shallows it may remain stationary for a while then its head will dart down to take its prey from the water. Sometimes, seeing a fish basking near the surface, the heron will move with long but very cautious strides to stalk it. In spite of its ungainly appearance this species frequently perches in trees.

Many things under and on the water are food to the heron. Fish, newts, tadpoles and frogs are taken as are water-voles and the young of aquatic birds.

Its most often heard note is a harsh, loud 'frarnk'. This is frequently made when the bird is in flight.

Although I have disturbed herons in reed-beds at night, I do not know whether any of them were roosting. Herons do sometimes feed in the hours between sunset and dawn. Most of them roost in tall trees.

*Swallow Family*

We have three representatives of this family. All are numerous in most parts of the British Isles, and catch their food while in flight.

*Swallow*

In April people with an interest in birds look out for swallows returning

Heron

from Africa. I have seen large numbers of them in the south of that continent during our winter.

At one time called chimney swallows, these birds are found near the habitations of men. Most frequent farm buildings and the open country around them, but others come to the suburbs and parks of towns.

The swallow is a blue-black bird, $7\frac{1}{2}$ inches (19 cm) from the tip of its beak to the end of its distinctively long tail streamers. Its under-parts are white, while its throat and forehead are red.

In flight, sometimes sweeping low over the surface of a pond to drink, or hawking close to the ground for insects disturbed by cattle, the swallow is unmistakable. Its forked tail with slender streamers is unlike that of any of our other land birds.

Insects of many sorts are snapped up in flight.

Its song, which is perhaps not as well known as it should be, is a short musical burble.

The pre-migration roosts of this species can be quite spectacular.

## House Martin
This species is similar to the swallow in its migrations, habitat and feeding methods.

It is only 5 inches (12·5 cm) long because it lacks the swallow's long tail streamers. In body size it is not very different from the swallow. A bluer bird, the whole of the under-parts and the lower back are pure white. The tail is forked.

The song of the house martin is weaker and less varied than the swallow's.

## Sand Martin
Upon their return from Africa the sand martins move up our main rivers. It is by them and lakes that one is most likely to see these birds.

Differing from the other swallows in being brown on the back and having a chest band of the same colour, this is also the smallest. $4\frac{3}{4}$ inches (12 cm) overall, it has white under-parts.

54

Although feeding in a similar way to our other two swallows, it does so more frequently over water and its flight is more fluttering.

When on the wing it has a pleasant short churring note and its song is very weak.

## Swift

One of the last of the birds to arrive in this country in spring and among the first to depart in autumn is the swift. It is of a different family to the swallows, although it may look somewhat similar.

Their main concentrations are near man's habitation, therefore swifts are commonly to be seen over town and village. However, they range widely for food and I have often seen them over remote moorlands.

Feeding on insects caught on the wing, these birds may be seen almost anywhere in this country apart from the northern parts of Scotland.

With a slender body $6\frac{1}{2}$ inches (16 cm) in length and long, curved, narrow wings, the swift has a very distinctive shape. It has a short, forked tail and apart from a white throat is uniformly brownish-black in colour. While the small, weak feet enable it to cling to vertical surfaces, they are no use for perching.

As its name implies, it is a fast flier. At times the wings appear to beat alternately rather than in unison. On an evening parties gather and dash around above the houses of village or town. It is then that their shrill notes are constant, making an exciting performance. Their control in flight is extremely accurate. Some swifts nesting in the roof of a small building used holes in the horizontal boarding below the eaves as entrances. These were 2 inches long and 1 inch wide. The birds coming in from feeding over a large lake swooped down and shot up through the holes at high speed. They did not touch the sides and I never saw one miss.

## Thrush Family

Among the commoner of our birds is the song thrush and this is the bird I have chosen as the first representative of its family.

Song thrush

## Song Thrush

Song thrushes may be seen at any time of the year, but as many leave us in autumn, there are fewer of them in winter. Of those that migrate many go to Ireland and others to France, Portugal and Spain.

🌳 You will find them in woods – broad leafed and coniferous – as well as in parks and gardens.

🐦🪶 They are some nine inches (23 cm) in length. Warm brown on the back and wings, they have buff on their breasts and flanks, while the black spots on the under-parts are longer than they are wide.

🐛 On the ground the thrushes' movements are brisk, progress being in short runs or series of hops. Earthworms and snails form the major part of their food. To obtain the first, the song thrush will sometimes be seen to make a short dash, halt with its head on one side, then suddenly grab the worm. Sometimes there is a lengthy tug-of-war before this is dragged from its burrow. With snails this

56

species is something of a specialist. Using a stone as an anvil, it holds the edge of the shell in its beak and batters it until it breaks. The thrush can then swallow the juicy body. It will return to the same stone many times and you may find one of these anvils surrounded by broken shells. None of the other members of the family of thrushes seem to have developed the habit.

You may hear song thrushes in song in about ten months of the year, the birds being silent in July and August. The peak period, when most thrushes are singing, is from the beginning of February to the end of May. No British bird has a more easily recognised voice. Perched in some tree it chooses a note or short phrase and repeats it, sometimes twice, but more often three or more times. Another note then receives the same treatment, to be followed by others. Although from bird to bird the songs vary as different phrases are used, the overall pattern of loud, clear notes being repeated makes the song unmistakable.

At night these thrushes roost in bushes and trees. Sometimes a few will sleep in the same group of laurels, but more often single birds will have their own chosen perches and in spring mated pairs may roost together.

## Mistle Thrush

Another thrush that is with us all the year is the mistle thrush; their numbers are about the same over the whole twelve months. Although some that breed with us move south after rearing their young, others move into this country from the Continent to winter with us.

This frequenter of open woodlands, hedgerows and orchards, originally got its name from the mistletoe, the berries of which it will take. It is sometimes called stormcock, from its habit of singing in the wildest weather.

About $1\frac{1}{2}$ inches (4 cm) longer than the song thrush, it is a greyer bird with its under-parts more strongly marked, the spots there being larger and rounder than those of that bird. When in flight the white underwings catch the eye, as do the white tips of the outer tail feathers as it alights.

Its actions on the ground are similar to those of the song thrush, although usually this bird stands more upright. In autumn, fruit and berries form a large part of its diet and family parties may be seen in the hedgerows. The young birds in their first feathers have a very speckled appearance.

It is mainly in the first five months of the year that we hear the song of the mistle thrush. As this is usually delivered from a high perch and is loud, it carries a long way. In style the song somewhat resembles that of the blackbird, but is much wilder, lacking the flute-like quality of the notes of that species. The loud jarring alarm note can best be imitated by quickly dragging a piece of wood across close-placed palings.

In autumn the family parties roost in bushes, but by the end of the year the birds choose their sleeping places singly or in pairs.

## Fieldfare

Although it is a rare breeding bird in the north of Britain it is as a winter visitor that we know this bird best. These thrushes come to us from their northern breeding grounds.

The flocks of fieldfares, sometimes large, are to be seen in autumn competing with the two species already described for the fruits and berries of the countryside. When these are all eaten they move to the open fields.

Almost the same size as the mistle thrush, their upper parts, particularly the head and lower back, are much greyer than those of that bird. The tail is almost black, the throat and breast rusty buff with black spots.

In shape and stance they resemble the mistle thrush and like it show light underwings when in flight. Their feeding habits are also similar to those of that bird.

Some of the fieldfare flocks are still with us in May and in that month I have occasionally heard birds singing. The song is a weak, disjointed effort, with many squeaky and chuckling notes in it. When in flight these large thrushes have a harsh 'ch-ch-chack, ch-ch-chack' call that is easily recognised.

Although during the hours of daylight fieldfares spend a good part of their time in trees, at night most of them roost in flocks on the ground.

## Redwing

Like the last described species, apart from a few pairs that breed in the north of Scotland, the redwing is a winter visitor to Britain. In fact it is not unusual to find both species in the flocks that move around the winter countryside.

In size, general appearance and habits, it resembles the song thrush. The most noticeable differences in plumage are the red flanks and the whitish lines over the eyes of the redwing.

The song is short and very variable. Outside the limited breeding area it is seldom heard in this country. There is one of the calls made by this species that it is very useful to know, and that is the contact note. When the birds are in passage these calls are frequently made. Particularly at night contact notes ensure that individuals do not stray from the flock. Not only does the 'see-ip' note of the redwing serve that purpose, but it also informs anyone listening, when the flocks are moving at night. Many times in the centre of a large city I have heard the calls and known that in the dark above me, the redwings were passing over, moving to other feeding grounds.

At night the communities roost in shrubberies, plantations and copses.

## Blackbird

This is the most numerous of our thrushes and is a common bird all the year round.

It is also the most frequently seen in towns. Defining its habitat is difficult as it is found on the lower slopes of mountains, in woodland, on farmland, in public parks and microscopic back gardens. Slightly bigger than the song thrush, the cock blackbird is easily described. He is all black with a bright yellow bill. The female is, however, dark brown, with a patch of a lighter shade on the throat. In its habits it behaves in much the same way as the song thrush. However, although some seem to be aware of the delicacy contained within the snail's shell, they have not learned how to get at it. Occasionally a blackbird will watch a thrush break a shell and then attempt to take the contents from it.

Hen blackbird feeding on frosted ground

The blackbird is justly famous for its song of flute-like quality. Americans I have taken birdwatching in spring have been amazed that we had a common bird that was such an accomplished singer. There is no way of doing justice to the mellow, if rather short warble, in words, but as it can be heard in almost any public park, it will soon be familiar to the reader. The loud cackling alarm call must also be well known. When the young are out of the nest, I hear it all day long, as the parents react to cats in the park I overlook from where I write.

Blackbirds are fond of evergreens as roosting places, but before they retire they often indulge in a period of loud 'chack-chacking'.

## Crow Family
Being large and black, the crows are a family of birds that have featured widely in folklore. There was a belief that a crow alighting on a house chimney foretold a death. That most people could not tell a crow from a rook did not seem to matter.

## Rook
This is a species that is to be seen in Britain throughout the year. Every-one must be familiar with their rookeries in spring and the sight of flocks

Rooks

of rooks in the winter fields.

🌳 Although they nest in trees, these are birds of the open farmland.

🐦 The rook is about eighteen inches (46 cm) in length and its plumage, beak and legs are black. Its feathers are glossy and iridescent. At the base of the slender bill is a bare patch, almost white, that extends down the throat. That is an aid to identification as none of our other crows have anything similar. When the rook is on the ground it can be seen that the shaggy looking feathers around the upper leg give a plus-four appearance. That is again distinctive of this species.

🐦 Communal in habit, rooks feed on the ground in flocks. Walking about rather sedately they extract grubs and worms from the earth and pick vegetable matter from its surface.

🐦 The cawing call of the rook has several variations, as you will hear if you stand near a rookery in spring.

Winter roosts sometimes contain vast numbers of birds. Usually they are situated in a wood of tall trees. Rooks converge on them from every direction. At and just before dusk, parties of various sizes straggle along the flight lines for upwards of fifteen miles. The window at which I write is near the centre of a large city. Late on a winter's afternoon, from it I can watch two flight lines that cross just to the south. The rooks on one are heading for a wood some eleven miles to the east. On the other, gulls are making their way northwards to a reservoir on the city boundary.

### Carrion Crow

Whatever the season there will be carrion crows in England, Wales and the southern half of Scotland. For most of the year they are solitary or in pairs, but in winter there are sometimes small flocks.

In addition to being found in open farming countryside, the carrion crow is not uncommon on the wild moorlands and fells.

About the same size as the rook, this crow is all black and has a heavier bill than that species. It lacks the rook's patch on the throat as well as the long feathers on the legs.

On the ground it will either walk or hop and sometimes makes longish jumps. As its name suggests, this bird will feed on the flesh of dead creatures. It will also kill small birds as well as taking the eggs and young of bigger species. In addition, it feeds on earthworms, beetles and seeds.

The voice of the carrion crow is harsher than the rook's and higher-pitched calls of greeting or anger are sometimes made.

When numerous, carrion crows have communal roosts in winter. The largest of these that I have known has held about a hundred birds.

### Jackdaw

This is another bird that stays with us all the year.

Its main haunts are old and ruined buildings, as well as woodlands where there are plenty of hollow trees.

A little smaller than the rook, the flocks of which it often joins, its

62

Jackdaw leaving its nest

under-parts are less densely black than those of that species. The back of the head is grey and its eyes are a pale shade of the same colour.

Its movements on the ground are more energetic and sprightly than those of the rook alongside which it feeds, although its food is similar.

It is from its call, sounding like Jack, that its name is derived.

Numbers of birds of this species will roost close to each other in crevices in cliffs, old buildings or hollow trees.

## Magpie
This is a resident bird.

It is particularly fond of woodland and country with tall hedgerows and is also found in towns.

At all times of the year its long tail and black and white plumage make the magpie easily identifiable.

Its rattling, chattering alarm is readily recognised.

63

The magpie is omnivorous, that means it will feed on almost any-thing, whether it be insect, vegetable or animal. In spring they rob birds' nests of eggs and young, and they will take small animals at any part of the year.

Gregarious by nature it sometimes roosts with either rooks or jack-daws, but groups of magpies will roost in trees away from other species.

*Finch Family*
This is a family of seed-eaters. Their bills are conical in shape and finches with the larger bills feed on the biggest seeds. In that way they are prevented from all competing for the same food and yet the full available range of seeds is used.

*Chaffinch*
This brightly coloured species stays with us in all seasons.

The chaffinch is a bird of woodlands, farmland and gardens.

Hen chaffinch

Six inches (15 cm) long, the cock is a brightly coloured bird: with pink cheeks and under-parts, slate blue cap, chestnut back and green rump, he is easily recognisable. His mate, olive-brown above and paler below, is less so, but both have white wing-bars and outer tail feathers that attract attention.

On the ground they walk with rather rapid steps or hop. The winter flocks that gather to feed in the fields are often of one sex. Their food consists of seeds, insects and their larvae, and some fruit.

The song, usually commencing about mid-February, rattles along gaily. As boys we put the words, 'In another month there comes the wheat-e-a-r', to it. The song varies in different parts of the country, much as human dialects do. In addition to the song, two call notes, a ringing 'spink, spink' and a rather dreary 'weet, weet', are well known. The last is supposed to foretell coming rain.

A hedgerow and shrubbery rooster in small parties outside the nesting season, chaffinches may also share bushes with greenfinches.

## Brambling

This rather chaffinch-like bird is a winter visitor from Scandinavia.

Bramblings feed, along with other finches and buntings, in the open fields and along woodside edges. When they first arrive a good place to look for them is where there are beeches. They are very fond of the seeds of that tree.

Its feeding and roosting habits are like those of the chaffinch and its song is rarely heard in this country. The cock – similar in shape to the chaffinch – has a dark brown head when in winter plumage and orange-rust shoulder patches. Both sexes have that colour on their breasts, also noticeable white rumps and wing-bars.

Bramblings have the typical undulating flight of finches.

## Goldfinch

Whether as one bird brightening a spring day with its cheerful song, in small parties feeding on autumn's thistle heads, or flocking in winter, the goldfinch is one of the most attractive of its family.

It is a bird of the country lanes, orchards and gardens. Smaller than the chaffinch, the gold from which it derives its name is in a broad bar on each of the black wings. The top of the head of the adult is also black, the face is red and the cheeks white. There are tawny-brown feathers on the rest of the body, except for the lower back which is very pale. Juveniles lack the striking pattern on the head and are sometimes called grey pates.

In flight the goldfinch looks light and bouncy. When feeding on the seeds of thistles they flutter around the heads like large moths. Most of their food is in the form of seeds obtained from growing weeds, but they also take insects and their larvae.

The song already mentioned has a liquid quality. So also has the contact note which is repeated frequently, both when the bird is flying and when it is perched.

This species roosts in trees in addition to bushes.

*Greenfinch*

Only slightly smaller than the chaffinch, the greenfinch is one of our resident birds.

Frequently to be seen in towns, it is also a bird of the country lanes and farmland.

Robust in build, the general colour of the cock greenfinch is, as one would expect, green, the under-parts being paler and more yellow than the upper. On the wings and by the sides of the tail are yellow patches which are very noticeable when the bird is in flight. The pale bill is more substantial than that of the chaffinch. There is less green in the rather drab plumage of the hen.

When feeding on the ground the greenfinch hops. Seeds of both wild and cultivated plants are eaten.

Most well known of the greenfinch's notes is the musical 'whe-e-e-e-ze' that makes one think of hot summer afternoons. That is probably because it is to be heard after most birds have ceased to sing. The spring song, that is delivered as the bird circles on slow-beating wings, has a jingling quality.

At night when returning from watching badgers, I have often disturbed numbers of these birds from the evergreens in which they like to roost.

*Linnet*

Nearly an inch (2·5 cm) shorter than the chaffinch, the linnet is with us the whole of the year.

Rough country suits it best, whether that be gorse-covered commons, moorland edges or neglected farmland.

In spring the cock is a very handsome bird with crimson on the head and chest. The back is chestnut, under-parts greyish-white and the tail near black. Lacking the red markings the female's plumage is more drab and is more streaked.

A hopping bird, the linnet perches on bushes rather than the branches of high trees. Its diet is mainly of seeds and in winter flocks of these birds search the fields for them.

When a party flies over, one often hears what sounds like twittering conversation. The song, that is usually sung from some exposed spray, lacks form, but has in it sweet and rather twanging notes.

Sometimes when walking across rough fields at night I have disturbed linnets that were sleeping on the ground amid rough grass and I have often come across them roosting in gorse.

*Tit Family*
*Blue Tit*

Familiar to most people, blue tits nest in spring in boxes placed on trees and walls in gardens and in winter feed on fat and nuts put out for them. Originally they were birds of the broad-leafed woodlands and most still live in that habitat, nesting in holes in trees.

One of our smaller birds, only $4\frac{1}{2}$ inches (11·5 cm) in length, the blue tit is well named. It is the only member of its family with bright blue crown, wings and tail. The face and forehead are white and there is a near black line through each eye; the back is greenish and the under-parts yellow.

When on the ground this species hops, but it obtains most of its food in trees. Its searches are brisk and energetic, even at times acrobatic, as it inspects the undersides of leaves and branches. It is there that it finds the insects, cocoons and caterpillars that make up a great part of its food.

The blue tit's song is high pitched and sibilant and its alarm a harsh 'chur-r-r-r'.

It roosts in holes in trees or in buildings.

### Great Tit
The great tit closely resembles the last described species in all aspects of behaviour and habitat.

Larger by an inch (2·5 cm) than the blue tit, its head and neck are a glossy blue-black, the cheeks being white. The under-parts are yellow and divided by a black line down the centre of the breast: this is the most easily identified characteristic. The upper-parts are greenish.

Few birds have a bigger variety of notes than the great tit. The late Ludwig Koch once told me that he had recorded eighty-seven variations. In spring its two-syllable song sounds at times bell-like, or rather like someone sharpening a saw and at others a singing 'teacher-teacher'. When alarmed its scolding note can sound somewhat like that of the blue tit.

### Warbler Family
We have many warblers and all of them except one rare species are summer visitors.

### Chiffchaff
This is the first of this family to arrive in spring.

The chiffchaff is a bird of woodlands and bushy areas.

Four and a quarter inches long (11 cm) this bird has upper-parts of drab, olive-brown and the underbody is white tinged with pale lemon-yellow. It has dark legs.

On the ground it hops, but it is most often seen in trees, where it systematically searches the leaves and branches. There it finds the insects, larvae and cocoons that are its food.

The song of the chiffchaff is often heard as early as March. It is a regular repetition of two musical notes and from it the bird gets its name. When alarmed it makes a rather plaintive pipe.

*Willow Warbler*
In everything except voice, this bird is very similar to the chiffchaff. It has the same sort of habitat.

Its plumage is like that bird's, but a little brighter and the willow warbler's legs are light coloured.

Feeding on insects, it searches for them in the same way.

The song – that is one of the most frequently heard in our countryside – is a sweet descending trill that finishes with a flourish. You need a good ear and plenty of practice to separate the willow warbler's alarm note from the chiffchaff's.

*Reed Warbler*
This is a bird of the reed-beds and is commonest south of the Humber.

Reed warbler

Three-quarters of an inch (1·9 cm) longer than the chiffchaff, the reed warbler is an even brown on the back and white with a buffish tinge beneath.

It spends nearly all its time in the thick phragmites reeds, often holding on the stems as shown in the illustration on page 69.

Like the rest of its family it feeds on insects.

The alarm note of the reed warbler has a churring quality. Made up of rather guttural notes interspersed with occasional sweet ones, the song is repetitive and can continue a long time without variations.

## Sedge Warbler

Any sort of wet place seems to satisfy the sedge warbler. I have found it by ditches as well as lakes and ponds.

About the same size as the reed warbler, it is easily distinguished by the white stripes above the eyes and the dark markings on the brown back.

It searches for insects in the same way, but is seen more often in osiers and bushes.

Although of a similar quality to that of the last described bird, the sedge warbler's song is more varied. The delivery is quicker and sometimes other species are mimicked.

## Wagtail Family
## Pied Wagtail

This bird is with us at all seasons.

Its habitat is less governed by the presence of water than is popularly supposed. Open countryside suits this bird and it is often to be seen near farm buildings.

Seven inches (18 cm) long – the tail being over a third of the total – the male is black and white. The face, belly, wing-bars and outer tail feathers are white and the rest black. There is grey on the back of the females and juveniles.

On the ground, where they are most often to be seen, wagtails run freely with the tail swinging up and down.

Sedge warbler.

 Their food is mainly insectivorous and they also take plants and seed.

Their rather simple twittering song is rarely heard. The normal call is a sharp 'chissick'.

Often roosting is communal. At one time the trees in O'Connell Street, Dublin, held a large winter roost.

*Yellow Wagtail*
Coming to Britain in spring this species spends its winters in Africa.

71

Hen yellow wagtail

🌳 The yellow wagtail is to be found in open country, hill pastures and marshes. I have seen them nesting miles from water on a Suffolk heath.

🐦🐦 About half an inch (1·3 cm) shorter than the pied this bird fully justifies the name yellow. From the base of its bill to the tail its under-parts are that colour. The upper-parts are olive-green, both wing and tail feathers are dark coloured, apart from the white outer feathers of the tail.

Its movement both on the ground and in flight are typically wag-tail, as is its food.

The flight call is longer than that of the pied wagtail.

## Grey Wagtail

This is a resident in these islands.

Seldom is this bird seen away from water. In spring and summer it is by the upper reaches of our rivers, while in winter it visits lakes and mud-fringed ponds.

Although this species is the same overall length as the pied, its very long black tail accounts for about half of the total. Yellow below and grey on the back, with black bib, the male is very handsome.

The female lacks the black on the throat.

Though in comparison with its relatives the tail of the grey wagtail is in perpetual motion, in other respects its behaviour and feeding habits are similar.

Like them it has a single note flight call, rather similar to that of the pied, and a simple, seldom heard song.

## Skylark

Our resident population is increased in winter by immigrants from the Continent.

Open fields, wolds and downs are the skylark's home.

Some 7 inches (18 cm) long, the streaky brown skylark is only likely to be confused with the woodlark. That bird is much more limited in distribution in this country, has white stripes over the eyes and a shorter tail. On the back the skylark is brown, but the dark centres of the feathers give it a streaked appearance. The chest is buff, heavily marked with a darker shade and the belly buffish-white. White feathers show at each side of the tail. The feathers of its crest are noticeable when raised to their full extent.

On the ground the skylark walks, but it is best known for its soaring song-flight and the sudden drop to earth at its completion.

Its food is varied, including insects, seed and some plants.

The song is a vigorous and prolonged repetition of a limited number of musical notes. It is powerful and carries well.

Often when crossing fields at night I have disturbed parties of roosting skylarks from the grass.

## Kestrel

Another bird we most often see in flight is the kestrel. This too is a resident.

It is a bird of open farmland, moor and city. This species has been very successful in moving into our towns and cities. In some of them its population density is as high, or higher, than in the surrounding countryside.

Thirteen inches (33 cm) long with pointed wings and long narrow tail, the kestrel has an anchor-like silhouette when in flight. The cock has a back of bright chestnut spotted with black. His head, lower back and tail are grey, the last tipped with a narrow band of white, preceded by a broad one of black. His mate is rufous above, buff below and heavily barred on the back.

One of the most distinctive things about the kestrel is its habit of hovering. Sometimes the wings beat rapidly, at others – where up-currents are created by a bank or cliff – they are near rigid and only the tail moves to maintain balance.

The alarm note is a high pitched 'ke-ke-ke'.

It roosts on cliffs, buildings or in trees.

## Tawny Owl

Resident and widespread, this is the commonest of our owls.

It is a woodland species which has also colonised towns and cities.

This 15 inch (38 cm) long bird has two colour phases. In one the upper-parts are tawny brown and in the other they are distinctly grey. They are flecked and barred with lighter and darker markings. The under-parts are buffish streaked with darker brown. In the greyish facial discs the eyes are dark.

Although sometimes seen hunting by day – particularly on winter afternoons – this is a bird of the night. The tawny owl has two main

Tawny owl

ways of catching its prey. One is to weave through the trees in silent flight low above the woodland floor and take its prey by surprise. Alternatively it will watch the ground from a low branch and plunge on to anything that moves or makes a sound.

Small mammals and birds form a great part of its food supply.

In addition to the well-known hoot a sharp sounding 'kewick' note is frequently heard.

Roosting by day this bird chooses holes in cliffs and trees in which to sleep; although sometimes you may find it doing so perched close to the trunk of a tree.

*Plover Family*
*Lapwing*
The lapwing is the best known, but the least typical of our plovers. It is the only one we have with broad wings and a crest.

75

Lapwing

It is a resident and its numbers are increased by a winter influx from the continent of Europe.

Open fields and moorland edges are the places to look for this species. In winter you will see them in large flocks.

In the air the lapwing's flapping flight, with slow wing-beats, is easily recognised. Normally it is rather wavering, but when the cock is displaying in spring it can be wildly acrobatic. Feeding on the ground it runs along with frequent pauses. Included in its food

76

are the larvae of many injurious insects, worms and vegetable matter.

The long crest of this 12 inch (30 cm) bird is an easy means of identification. That, along with the top of the head, throat and upper chest is black; apart from the pinkish-beige feathers beneath the tail the under-body is white. Although looking black at a distance, the back is dark green with some purplish iridiscence.

It is from its call that the lapwing has been given such vernacular names as peewit, puit and tuit. These describe a cry that can vary in pitch and intensity, according to whether the bird is displaying or showing concern for its young.

## Golden Plover

In the breeding season this bird is to be found on moorlands, but it leaves them for the valleys and coastal mudflats in winter.

An inch (2·5 cm) shorter than the lapwing, it is more trim and less bulky in shape. With bullet head and pointed wings it is a typical plover. The dark coloured upper-parts are liberally speckled with gold in the breeding season. In the same season the face, throat and belly are black. The extent of the black varies considerably with individual birds. On a well marked bird, it covers all but a narrow band of paler feathers that separate it from the upper-parts. Sometimes – particularly with hens – the black area is reduced to a line down the throat and a black belly. There is no black plumage in winter and the back is duller.

Like all our plovers the golden runs and walks on the ground and does not perch.

Although the larvae, etc., are not necessarily of the same species, its food is similar to the lapwings.

The spring song, delivered while the bird is in flight, is a repetition of long musical rather melancholy notes. Liquid in quality, the call note has many variations to suit differing circumstances.

## Waders

This is not the name of a family, but is used for describing a large group of birds of somewhat similar habit. I have chosen widely differing species for my examples.

Curlews

## Curlew

Like the golden plover, the curlew moves from moorland to shore and back again as the seasons change.

This is the largest of our waders being nearly 2 feet (60 cm) long. Its plumage is pale brown speckled with darker brown. The under-parts are paler than the back. Size, a long, down-curved bill and long legs make this an easily identified bird.

Stalking along with long strides on the moor it collects insects and some berries – on the shore it feeds on shrimps, molluscs, small crabs, etc.

The richly musical call sounds somewhat like its name and the rapid, bubbling song is sung by the curlew in descending flight.

## Oystercatcher

A bird of the shore at all seasons, its numbers are greatly increased by migrants in winter.

Medium among the waders in size, some seventeen inches (43

78

cm) in length, the oystercatcher is black and white. The white is, apart from the wing-bands, restricted to the under-parts. The orange-red bill and pink legs are long and brightly coloured.

Walking along the shore and over rocks, it feeds on shellfish of many kinds.

The normal call is a clear 'cleep' pipe and the song is a similar note repeated at rapidly increasing speed.

*Snipe*
The snipe is with us all the year round.

Being a bird of the marshes and bogs it is widespread where they are.

Just over 10 inches (25 cm) long, it is a brown bird with both darker and lighter markings. The under-parts are a warm buff. A pale mark along the head divides the black crown and with the light stripes that curve over the eyes gives the whole a strongly

striped appearance. Both the straight bill and the legs are long.

When disturbed the snipe flies away in zig-zag flight that is unmistakable. With the slender bill – the tip of which is very sensitive – it probes in the mud for food, extracting both animal and vegetable matter.

It is usual for a snipe that has been put up to give a loud 'scarp' call. The song is mechanical, being created by the air playing on the outer tail feathers – held at right angles to the body – as the flying bird descends at speed. A loud drumming sound is produced.

*Gull Family*
*Black-headed Gull*
Although gulls are usually looked upon as seabirds a large proportion of our black-headed gulls are to be found inland. Many never see the sea. Even in our cities they are to be seen at all seasons.

Coastal dunes, marshes both by the sea and inland, farmland and cities, all have their populations of this species.

This is the smallest of our resident gulls, being 15 inches (38 cm)

Black-headed gull

long. In summer its head is dark chocolate brown, but this characteristic is lost in winter. Soon after breeding is finished the dark feathers are moulted to leave a noticeable spot behind each eye. The black wing-tips, grey back and white body are retained all the year. Both beak and legs are coral-red. When the bird is flying a narrow wedge of white, with its base at the wing-tips, is noticeable on the leading edge of each wing.

In flight they seem more buoyant than other gulls and on the ground more energetic.

It also varies from the others in having a high-pitched, skirling call, more like the voices of terns than gulls.

Almost any food from scraps to carrion is swallowed.

The black-headed gull roosts on reservoirs, sometimes in thousands (see projects on page 94) and on the ground.

### Herring Gull
This is the best known of our coastal gulls and is common inland in winter – both on farmland and city dump. Although non-breeding birds are also there in summer, most are by the sea.

Herring gull in winter

Medium in size, it is some 22 inches (56 cm) from the tip of its bill to the tail end. Apart from the grey back and black wing-tips, this bird's plumage is white. The legs are flesh-coloured, the bill yellow, with a red patch on the lower mandible. In winter the head is streaked with grey. See the illustration on page 81.

In flight it frequently glides and on the ground has a rather sedate walk.

Feeding as it does on farmland, rubbish dumps and sewage outfalls, almost any food is acceptable to this species.

Sleeping on cliff ledges in summer, for the rest of the year it has similar behaviour to the black-headed gull.

## Water Birds
### Moorhen

On any day in the year this species is to be found on the borders of ponds or slow-moving rivers.

This sooty-black bird is 13 inches (33 cm) long. Its most easily recognised features are the outer white feathers of its otherwise black under-tail. Another noticeable characteristic is the red of the forehead and the base of the bill. The legs are green.

When the moorhen is swimming, the head and tail are moved in a jerky action, as though they were both on the same camshaft. As it walks – rather deliberately – it frequently flicks up the tail. With both actions the white outer tail feathers are brought into prominence.

Perhaps the best known note of this species is a harsh 'coorrk'.

Although the moorhen is often seen swimming, most of its food is found at the side of the water. It will also feed in the surrounding fields. The food is mainly vegetable, but some insects, caterpillars, worms and seed are taken.

### Coot

This species is resident and it is often found in the same places as the last.

Another similarity is that they both have near-black plumage. However at 15 inches (38 cm) the coot is longer and it is also

Coot – note its lobed toes.

noticeably more plump. The tail is rather short, but the white forehead plate and bill cannot be overlooked.

 It may be because the feet are large and the toes lobed, but when walking this bird puts them down with apparent care. Very good swimmers, coots dive for the water weeds that form the main part of their food. Larvae and water snails – probably on the weeds – are also eaten.

In addition to peevish-sounding croaks this species has some short sometimes almost explosive notes.

*Duck Family*
Although ducks are associated with water they have a variety of feeding habits. Surface-feeding ducks sift the mud by the water's edge, diving ducks collect their food from under the water; some species graze and the sawbills catch fish. As I am dealing with the commoner species I will only describe two surface feeders and one diving duck.

*Mallard*
As with all the ducks in this section, numbers increase in winter as migrants join our resident birds.

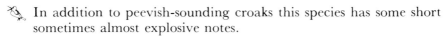 Marshes, ditches, slow-moving rivers, lakes and ponds – par-

ticularly those with muddy margins – attract mallard.

This large, nearly 2 feet (61 cm) long, duck is our commonest and is often seen on lakes in public parks. In the breeding season the drake has a dark green, glossy head, a narrow white collar round the neck and his breast is purple-brown. The back is ashy-brown with darker markings and white that give the effect of broad stripes. Above the grey under-parts there is a purple wing patch (speculum), margined by black and white on the wings. The rump, with its distinctive curly feathers, is black, the tail white. Mottled brown, the female has a similar speculum. After the breeding season the drake goes into eclipse, his plumage resembling that of the female.

The mallard walks with the typical duck waddle and has powerful flight.

Its voice is like that of its farmyard relatives.

Feeding by sifting mud, or up-ending in shallow water, the mallard obtains both insect and vegetable food.

## Teal
To be found at the same sort of places as the last species.

This is the smallest of our ducks, being only 14 inches (35·5 cm) in length. Although the head markings of the drake are striking in a picture, they are difficult to see, even at a moderate distance, when the light is poor. In those circumstances I find the easiest way to identify him is by the white line above the edge of the folded wing and the creamy triangle beneath the tail. The feathers of the head are chestnut; around the eyes and tapering towards the back, are elongated commas of dark green outlined in yellow. Both the upper part of the mantle and the flanks are grey, the rest of the back being brownish as are the flight feathers, and the speculum is green. The female is a rather dark brown mottled bird with under-parts paler in winter than summer.

The most often heard note is a conversational pipe that is made by birds feeding among the reeds. This call enables them to keep in contact when out of sight of each other.

84

Male tufted duck

*Tufted Duck*

A diving duck; this bird prefers the deeper lakes and spends more time on the water than the previous two.

All black except for the flanks and belly that are white, in the breeding season the drake is a striking bird. He is some 17 inches (33 cm) in length. At that time of the year he also has a long drooping crest. His mate is a dark brown bird with light under-parts and a short tuft of feathers at the back of the head. In eclipse the adult male resembles her, but is darker coloured.

The duck has a growling note, and when displaying the drake whistles softly.

Birds of this species have been known to dive to depths of about 16 feet (5 metres), for the small fish, molluscs and insects that are their staple diet.

## What, where and when to watch

When you have learned to recognise most of the birds near your house, you will wish to see other species. That will mean visiting different habitats. Nature and bird reserves are ideal places for seeing birds. Remember that they are not zoos and the birds you wish to see may not show themselves. You may be able to get your parents to take you to some of the places of special interest. Sometimes I go on trips with the local R.S.P.B. group, and parents who are members bring their children along.

It is not only necessary to know where to go, but it is important to know when. Sometimes the timing is critical. For instance, for a birdwatcher, one of the most exciting sights is that of vast numbers of waders on or over the shore. That is not to be seen in summer because most of the birds in the flocks are winter visitors. The best times are between November and March, although sites where the waders congregate before moving north early in April can be very good. At low tide at most of the places where these birds gather, there are many acres of sand and mud. Over this the flocks scatter widely and as there is no cover on an open shore, they are difficult to approach. When the tide comes in the birds retreat before it and as more and more of their feeding grounds are covered by the sea, they are driven on to rocks, ridges and banks of sand still above the water. Not only does the advancing tide bring the birds closer to the observer, but as the sea covers more of the banks, birds take off and in large flocks fly around before those unable to find somewhere to alight head for inland fields. There they settle to await the turn of the tide. Therefore it pays to arrive before and wait through the period of high water. Tide tables can be obtained from stationers and bookshops near the coast. If you live inland similar shops can get the one your require for a few pence. At most reference libraries, the Admiralty Table which gives times for the whole coastline can be consulted.

There are other bird sights and sounds that only last for short periods of the day, but generally it is enough to know the right season. That the birdwatcher and the bird should be at the same place at the same time, is the first principle of birdwatching.

Throughout the British Isles there are numbers of nature and bird reserves, while around the coasts and on small islands are bird observatories. They are owned or managed by several different bodies. The access conditions vary a great deal, at some of them one can walk straight in, at others you pay at the entrance and at some one must be accompanied by a warden. In some cases booking in advance is necessary. That is particularly important when wishing to visit islands.

The reserves nearest your home are most likely to be owned or managed by the county Naturalists Trust. First find where the Trust's headquarters are – the library or your school might help – then contact them. You can ask for the locations of their reserves and find out about being allowed to visit them.

The R.S.P.B. owns and manages most of Britain's bird reserves. If you are a member of the Y.O.C. (see Joining a Society) you will receive information about them, if not you will require to write to The Royal

Society for the Protection of Birds, The Lodge, Sandy, Bedfordshire SG19 2DL.

In addition to Slimbridge, the Wildfowl Trust have several other reserves; at all of them there is an emphasis on wildfowl. Information can be obtained from the Trust at Slimbridge, Gloucestershire.

At the bird observatories there is usually simple overnight or weekly accommodation, so that those workers interested in migration can stay. Some on islands are inaccessible to the casual visitor, but others on the mainland can be visited. If in doubt write to the observatory.

In the space at my disposal I can only mention a limited number of reserves and their special interests. My aim is to suggest where to see what birds and when, but because I mention a bird at a place in a certain season, that does not always mean that is the only place or time to see it.

*Spring*

Even before the calendar says it is spring, the first of our returning migrants are beginning to arrive on our coasts. Although most of them are busier in autumn, this is an exciting time at the observatories. As many of the arriving birds as possible are trapped, and if they have numbered rings on their legs, the numbers are recorded in order that the birds' histories may be traced. Any birds without rings are ringed in the hope that they will eventually be caught again and it will then be known to where they have travelled. As the season advances more and more migrants arrive and along with them birds that will travel farther north. As Val has mentioned, many birdwatchers go to these places to look for the rarities that occur.

Some of the favoured observatories are:

Slapton Ley, Devon
Portland Bill, Dorset
Beachy Head, Sussex
Romford Sewage Farm, Essex
Walberswick, Suffolk
Gibraltar Point, Lincolnshire
Spurn Point, Yorkshire
Teesmouth, Durham
Walney, Lancashire

There are many more, and in addition some of the promontories on our coasts – particularly south and east – are recognised migration watch points.

Most of us think of spring as the time of birdsong, but overlook the fact that many birds make noises that by our standards are not musical. That does not mean that the sounds are unwelcome. When bitterns began booming their weird note in East Anglia early in this century, the sound thrilled people interested in birds. These birds had been absent from Britain as breeding birds for several years and it was good to have them back. Now the bittern is re-established and has extended its range. Its voice can be heard and sometimes the bird can be seen at Minsmere and Leighton Moss R.S.P.B. Reserves. The first of these is in Suffolk and the other in Lancashire. Both have extensive areas of water and large reed-beds. Amid the close growing reed stems where the bitterns nest, sedge and reed warblers sing. On the lagoons are many aquatic species and overhead you may see that rare bird, the marsh harrier. Passage birds drop in at both to add to the interest. Now avocets return to Minsmere each year and may be watched from the permanent hides.

Places where thousands of seabirds nest are most exciting to visit and there are many of these on our coasts, although there are very few cliff colonies between the Isle of Wight and the mouth of the Humber. One of the finest is on Bempton Cliffs, not far from Bridlington in Yorkshire. Off the coast of Northumbria are the Farne Islands where one can walk along paths bordered by nesting terns, as well as see close-packed cliff nesters. Two other famous tern colonies are at Scolt Head and Blakeney Point in north Norfolk.

On the West Coast a large number of lesser black-backed gulls nest on Walney Island, Lancashire. Terns and gulls breed at Ravenglass and there is a colony of cliff nesters at St Bees Head. Both the last two places are in Cumbria.

Scotland, Northern Ireland and Wales have many miles of sea cliffs on which there are seabird colonies, but I have only room for the most famous. Handa off the coast of Sutherland has breeding great skuas in addition to the birds on the cliff ledges. Ailsa Craig west of Girvan and the Bass Rock in the Firth of Forth have large numbers of gannets. Rathlin Island and parts of the adjacent coastline of Northern Ireland have choughs as well as seabirds. Off the Welsh coast the group of islands Skomar, Skokholm and Grassholm, with populations ranging from gannets to Manx shearwaters, are tremendously interesting.

There are plenty of places to go in spring but remember that the woods, fields and lanes around where you live are then the haunt of birds that have been absent all winter.

The meeting of two habitats – woodland and farm fields

*Summer*

In some ways this is the most difficult season for the birdwatcher. Small birds are frequently hidden from view among the dense foliage on the trees and the thick vegetation on the ground. In addition, there are many juvenile birds on the branches and their plumages and calls can be difficult to identify. Birdwatching in lanes can be productive at this season. Settle in a suitable place and watch. Birds frequently cross the lane as they fly from one bush to another.

In July birdsong is dwindling, but reed, sedge, garden warblers and blackcaps are to be heard. If you know any commons or heaths, you can visit them at dusk to listen for the nightjar's churring song. It sounds rather like a two-stroke motorcycle in the distance. On the telephone wires by the lanesides corn buntings and yellow hammers continue to sing until the end of August.

The first of the migrants moving south travel down the country. As many of these feed by the water, watching by lakes, ponds and at old-style sewage farms will yield good results at this period. This is a good time to go to any reserve which has hides overlooking water, particularly if that has margins of open mud. Alternatively, try to find a suitable place near your home and hide close to it. The birds to look out for are wood and

One of the great pleasures of birdwatching is the attractive scenery to which it takes you

green sandpipers, greenshanks, ruffs and grey phalaropes.

The summer can be a very dry period. If you live in a part of the country where rivers and lakes are few and far between, by watching some pond where birds drink, you can sometimes see species that you did not know were in the area. A pond close to woodland will probably give the best results. Birds like crossbills, that spend most of their time in the tops of conifers and shy, elusive hawfinches may put in appearances.

Another feature of this period is the flocking of some species. On the moors curlews gather together before departing for the coast, where they will spend the winter. Golden plovers move from the hills to share lowland fields with the large flocks of lapwings. When moving down to the valleys, golden plovers have favourite fields where they congregate. I have known them use the same one for many years in succession. Black-headed gulls – many having already lost the dark hood of spring – gather where the soil is being broken. Family parties of many species, from long-tailed tits to mistle thrushes, are to be seen in bushes and trees.

### Autumn

This is a very busy season on our coasts. Many birds that will stay here through the winter make their landfall on the East coast and others on their way to Africa pass down it. In the estuaries of all our shores, the wintering flocks of waders begin to collect.

At places like the Isle of May in the Firth of Forth, Teesmouth, Spurn

Point, Gibraltar Point and Walberswick, large numbers of passage birds are ringed. The actual placing of the numbered ring on a bird's leg can only be done by a qualified ringer. Information about the ringing scheme can be obtained from the British Trust for Ornithology who organise it; their address is Beech Grove, Tring, Hertfordshire. At the observatories and recognised migration look-out points, you will find experts at identification and they will recognise rarities you might well miss.

Of course all migration is not along the coast. Towards the end of summer a steady stream of warblers trickles down the country. These small birds do not move as a flock, but pass along on a broad front. If you are patient and watch carefully at a suitable spot, you will find there is a steady flow. Your first clue may be a short song that sounds like a faint echo of the spring music. That is the time to watch and listen. If you are lucky, you will see other warblers of the same species following the southward trail. You do not necessarily require to be in the country to be aware of this movement. Moving from tree to tree and garden to garden, these small birds cross cities.

In September the swallows are preparing to migrate. During the day you see them gathering in groups on telephone wires and house tops. At some places, like Chichester Harbour in Sussex, large flocks of sand martins collect. Some years vast numbers of swallows and sand martins roost in the reed-beds at Fairburn Ings in Yorkshire. There is nothing permanent about these gatherings, and after having been used for several years, a place may for some reason become unsuitable and another be chosen. Therefore, keep a sharp lookout for changes in your own area.

At home you can start to put out food to attract birds to your garden. Wherever that is placed, make sure it is so sited that cats cannot approach it unseen. Bird-tables on posts or to hang can be bought, very often gardening centres sell them, but you can build your own. Peanuts, which will attract many species, are now sold in sausage-shaped net bags. These, when hung up, ensure that birds only take away small portions of food. Household scraps, particularly fatty ones, and corn, can be placed on the bird-table. Mixed corn for wild birds can be bought in packets, but some pet shops mix their own. Water is also important and birds must be able to perch comfortably on the edge of the container.

## Winter

The flocks of fieldfares and redwings from Scandinavia spread over the fields and by the edge of the wood bramblings feed on the beech mast. On our lakes an influx of birds from Europe increases the numbers of ducks.

New species such as golden eye and smew appear, goosanders and mergansers are seen in numbers south of their breeding range. In the estuaries and bays along the coast waders and geese congregate.

This is a good time to visit the World Wildlife Reserves. At all of them the ducks in the pens are in their best plumage. Looking at these captive birds at close quarters, you can note details that will enable you to identify them in the wild. The presence of these birds attracts wild ones and there are usually plenty flying around.

At Slimbridge in Gloucestershire, large flocks of wild Bewick's swans and white-fronted geese gather in winter and can be watched from hides. In Lancashire at Martin Mere, many wildfowl come into the lagoons and on the merse at Caerlaverock on the Solway Firth, a large number of barnacle geese gather. Although I have seen small parties of this handsome goose at various places, it was at Caerlaverock I learned to know it well. Since then I have visited Islay in the Inner Hebrides where there are as many as 20,000 of these birds in winter.

Not far north of the Solway is Loch Ken. Near to it I have seen the Greenland white-fronted goose as well as greylag geese. On its waters pintail and whooper swans add variety. The whole area is good for geese, greylags and pinkfeet can be often seen from the road.

On the Humber and around the Wash pink-footed geese are reasonably common. Farther south brent geese in large numbers feed along the coasts of Norfolk and Essex. These are usually of the dark-bellied race. At Strangford Lough in Northern Ireland there are large flocks of the more striking pale-bellied brent geese.

On the coast massed manoeuvres by thousands of waders – in Morecambe Bay I have seen 40,000 knot in one flock – are quite spectacular. Morecambe Bay is one of the best places to see them, but there are many other bays where they can be enjoyed. Also on the coast we find snow buntings searching among the tide-wrack, while with luck we may see shore larks in the fields close to it.

Probably because of the failure of their food supply, we sometimes have invasions of large numbers of some of the northern species. Usually these are first noticed on the coast and then spread through the country. Some years we get much larger numbers of waxwings or crossbills than usual. What did come as a surprise was the arrival of large numbers of nutcrackers, a bird that does not usually winter here.

Winter is the time to put up nesting-boxes. By spring the birds will be used to seeing them. I am sure that long before nesting material is gathered, birds prospect possible sites and visit them regularly. If you already have next-boxes they can be cleaned and any necessary repairs carried out. When putting up new boxes avoid positioning them in such a way that they face south. Young birds in a box on which the sun shines all day can suffer considerable discomfort and possibly die from the heat.

The most popular boxes are those for tits. These have entrance holes $1\frac{1}{8}$ inches (29 mm) in diameter. To prevent woodpeckers, grey squirrels or other predators from enlarging the hole in order to get at the young or eggs, tin can be fixed around it. This should be done in such a way that the nesting birds do not injure themselves as they enter and leave.

Before winter's official end herons, ravens, crossbills and some thrushes have started to nest. From January onwards fulmars visit their nesting cliffs and by the end of February other seabirds are doing so. Wheatears and chiffchaffs arrive on the South coast before spring and many of our resident birds are in full song.

## Projects

What can you do in addition to learning to identify birds?

First you can make lists. Normally you would keep a list of birds seen and add each new sighting to it. Why not keep lists of birds seen on each car or train journey? If you are travelling a long way you will find it an exciting way to pass the time. When you have a friend, brother or sister with you it would be fun to combine; each trying to be the first to see and identify a species. You can also make lists of birds seen in your garden, local park, on your way to school and when on holiday. If carefully kept, the interest to be found in the lists will increase as you get more and more for comparison.

One very interesting experiment you can do, is to find a suitable park, woodland or lane near your home and compare the species to be seen there all the year round. The best way to do this is to visit the place regularly, daily or weekly will do, and walk along a fixed route, noting each bird you see. Each visit should be at the same time of the day and you should not deviate from the chosen route. Decide on some time that you can keep clear for this project, either each day or one day a week. If the last, use the same time and day each week. Note down each bird as you see it. It is a good idea to have a card with the names of the more common species on it, then all that is needed is a mark beside the name. If you wish you can use the standard symbol of sex, for those species where the plumage of the male differs from the females. The line below indicates my meaning.

BLACKBIRD ♀♂♂♀♂♀♂        Total 4 males, 3 females

When you see a new species its name will be written on the card. In that way not only will your notes eventually show you how the species in the habitat vary throughout the year, but also any variations in the sex ratio of some of them. If carried out properly over a year, such a survey can provide quite a lot of information; for instance, it should show what migrants arrive or depart and when. Your notes will indicate which birds remained in the area and which moved on. Weather can affect bird populations and you can note rises and falls due to it. Another thing is that consistent regular watching of an area often shows the presence of species that could be overlooked on a single visit.

I have mentioned the flight lines of certain birds flying to winter roosts. In the case of the rooks I see from my window, some of my friends first traced them to their roost, then back again to their feeding grounds. They did that by watching the flying birds and noting some landmark in the distance that they passed. The following evening they were at that landmark and watched the birds fly past another farther on. By making steps forward each evening they eventually came to the roost. While there they found that birds were coming to it from all points of the compass. Using the same method in reverse they traced the birds along several lines to feeding places the other side of the city. If you see birds flying on regular flight lines early in the morning, or in the evening, you can try to find where they come from and where they are going.

You can follow that technique to find out where gulls roost. Near towns this is likely to be on reservoirs. On them gulls – particularly in autumn – congregate in their thousands. Having found the roost there are all sorts of things that you can do. You can count the birds regularly to find when peak numbers occur. If you do so for each species, you will probably discover that most, if not all, the lesser black-backed gulls leave before winter. Should there be any other large stretches of water near, you can check whether they are used. You can then find if any that are have their own populations or whether birds change from one to the other. If there are surrounding fields these can be checked for roosting birds.

When we fall asleep our muscles relax and if we did so while standing we would fall. With birds it is quite the reverse; when the claws are wrapped around a branch and the weight of the body settles on the legs, the muscles tighten. Without any effort the bird can remain safely perched throughout the night. In winter when there are no leaves on the bushes, you may use a torch to find birds sleeping in them. Make as little disturbance as possible and only use the torch sparingly. If you do not disturb the bird it may continue to use the roost and it will be possible to watch for its arrival each evening.

In daylight you can search the trunks of Wellingtonias for the cavities excavated by treecreepers. You can also inspect the bark of other trees, for the natural crevices in which tits and other small birds sleep. White droppings on the bark of the tree below the cavity will often indicate those in use.

Some years ago I worked with others on a starling enquiry. A group of us visited a village once a week at dusk. We spread out so that every building in it could be seen by at least one of us. It did not take long to find all the roosting places and later we proved that most were used throughout the year. Can you find out where the birds around your house retire to sleep?

## Joining a society

Although most towns now have birdwatching clubs, not many of them have junior sections. There is one national society that is for young people up to fifteen years old, that is the Young Ornithologists Club. This is organised by the Royal Society for the Protection of Birds and the address is given on page 87. In many towns there are leaders who will take members of this club out for walks or on organised outings. There are also a variety of birdwatching holidays for members. In the care of capable adults and experienced birdwatchers, groups spend holidays in a wide variety of habitats. There are also opportunities for combining birdwatching with some other outdoor activity such as sailing or pony trekking.

The Y.O.C. has its own magazine and each member receives it periodically. In addition, various types of competitions are organised.

Many towns and cities have a R.S.P.B. representative and your librarian is likely to know that person's name and address. The local representative will be able to let you know whether there is a Y.O.C. leader in your area. If you do not have one, you can obtain details of membership from the R.S.P.B.

Some schools have their own natural history societies. If you have several schoolmates also interested in birdwatching, why not approach one of your teachers and request that a group should be formed? A possible alternative would be to ask a youth-leader, Sunday-school teacher or scoutmaster to form one. The R.S.P.B. sends information to schools and any adult person forming a group would receive assistance and information on request.

# Index of Birds Named

Pages in **heavy type** indicate a main entry in the identification guide